Praise for
The Global Consultant
How to Make Seven Figures Across Borders

The more I listen to Alan Weiss, the more I learn. From practical lessons such as finding the real buyer within an organization; creating a proposal with the client as a peer; "closing" the deal without ambiguities. To life changing lessons such as TAABBITO (there's always a bigger boat in the ocean); enhancing one's self-esteem, perhaps the biggest problem facing all of us; real wealth is discretionary time. Alan's teachings, coupled with my own skills in my field of expertise, have enabled me to be a better consultant to lawyers all across the United States, Canada, Australia and England. Alan Weiss has the skills to teach sophisticated lessons in the real world in a straightforward and understandable language. If language controls the discussion, and discussion controls the relationship, and relationships control the business, Alan is the master.

Edward Poll, J.D., M.B.A., CMC
President, LawBiz® Management

Imagine leaving a job as a high school maths teacher and within 24 months earning a six-figure income coaching executives at companies like McDonald's, Coca-Cola, and Marriott, some of whom were responsible for more than a billion dollars worth of revenue. When I left my high school teaching position, all I had was passion and an ability to work with people to improve results. Alan Weiss taught me an overall framework with detailed suggestions on how to provide value-added marketing to attract great clients and provide value to clients to sustain great relationships. Buy *The Global Consultant* immediately and apply the practical ideas in it.

Dan Coughlin
President, The Coughlin Company
Author of ACCELERATE: 20 Practical Lessons
to Boost Business Momentum

In this book, Alan Weiss and Omar Khan show experienced global consultants as well as newcomers how to expand not only their brand and expertise but also their markets! Alan has parlayed his incomparable experience in terms of consulting all over the world—and here he shares those "million dollar consulting" secrets for global success. Omar is the ultimate *sensei* for anyone wanting to succeed globally. His company Sensei is a leader in leadership development consulting from the Americas to Asia Pacific. When either of these guys speaks about global consulting, listen carefully! When they come together... smart people not only listen to their advice, they act on it!

Ron Kaufman
Author, UP Your Service!
Founder and President, UP Your Service College

Omar straddles multiple cultures and disciplines naturally. His advice and the experiences he shares crosses national boundaries and helps people understand the world and how to thrive in it as a consultant, as a leader both in and outside of the scope of business. Omar brings a very unique approach of genuineness to each and every person he meets. As a leader of Powered by Professionals, I've been grateful and excited to work personally with Omar to see the applicability of his global experience and expertise for everyone from young leaders of college age, to CEOs and thought leaders throughout the world in for profit and non-profit organizations. Certainly he's one of the first people I go to for help to take our business to new levels of success nationally and internationally. He also works with me on a personal basis to prepare me for the challenges of a very stressful business and keeps me on track to fulfill my desire to live a fully abundant life.

Ken Grosso
CEO, Powered By Professionals

The Global Consultant

How to Make Seven Figures Across Borders

The Global Consultant

How to Make Seven Figures Across Borders

Alan Weiss, Ph.D.
Author
Million Dollar Consulting

Omar Khan
Author
Liberating Passion: How The World's
Best Global Leaders Get Winning Results

John Wiley & Sons (Asia) Pte. Ltd.

Copyright © 2009 Alan Weiss and Omar Khan
Published in 2009 by John Wiley & Sons (Asia) Pte. Ltd.
2 Clementi Loop, #02-01, Singapore 129809

This publication is designed to provide accurate and authoritative information
in regard to the subject matter covered. It is sold with the understanding that
the publisher is not engaged in rendering professional services. If professional
advice or other expert assistance is required, the services of a competent professional person should be sought.

Other Wiley Editorial Offices

John Wiley & Sons, Inc., 111 River Street, Hoboken, NJ 07030, USA

John Wiley & Sons, Ltd., The Atrium, Southern Gate, Chichester, West Sussex
P019 8SQ, UK

John Wiley & Sons (Canada), Ltd., 5353 Dundas Street West, Suite 400,
Toronto, Ontario M9B 6H8, Canada

John Wiley & Sons Australia Ltd., 42 McDougall Street, Milton, Queensland
4064, Australia

Wiley-VCH, Boschstrasse 12, D-69469 Weinheim, Germany

Library of Congress Cataloging-in-Publication Data

ISBN: 978-0-470-82386-6

Typeset in 11/13 point, Plantin Light by C&M Digitals (P) Ltd.
Printed in Singapore by Saik Wah Press Pte. Ltd.

Contents

Dedication   xi
Acknowledgments   xiii

Introduction   1

I. The Worldview   3

1. Why Go Global?
   *Because it's as easy to consult in Kuala Lumpur
   as it is in Kansas*   5

   The earth isn't flat, it's right here   6
   We are more alike than apart   8
   Harsh truth: American English, American dollar,
      American knowledge   12
   Capitalism compels collaboration   15

2. Projecting Expertise and Building Relationships
   How to be nearby from 8,000 miles away   19

   The trick to projecting expertise:
      First get the right type   19
   Breaking in is relatively easy to do   22
   Once you've got the relationships,
      keep connecting   24
   Amplifying the impact of your brand and
      presence: Adapting to local needs   27

3. Creating International Presence
   Alliances and the appeal of the knowledge exporter   33

   What Drucker said   33
   The local alliance   37

Physical presence   40
The local, formal office   44

II. The Itinerary   49

4. Requisites for Success: Material
   Creating your own time machine   51

   Staying on top of your game   51
   17 ways to stay mentally and physically fit   52
   You don't have to be a pack animal   55
   When things go "bump" in the night   58
   There's feeling good and looking good   62

5. Requisites for Success: Personal
   Educating yourself   69

   Education basics: Before advising others,
       let's teach ourselves how to get things done   70
   Educating yourself for success:
       Understanding countries and people   74
   Educating yourself for life: Lifelong learning   79
   Educating habits: Global credibility   83

6. Requisites for Success: New Paradigms
   Creating global value   85

   Creating new value   86
   Make sure you know what you've got   89
   To make a global impact, build momentum   91
   Decide how you want to deliver value   94
   Make it easy   97

   Interlude
   Travelogue   101

   Omar   101
   Alan   110

III. **The Journey** 117

7. Applying Value-Based Fees
   Your time is not the issue and had better not be 117

   The philosophy of value-based fees 119
   The fundamentals of value-based pricing 123
   Overcoming objections and creating converts 126
   Using value-based pricing internationally 129

8. Adding Value Across Cultural Distinctions
   What you shouldn't adapt is as important
   as what you should 133

   Experience it yourself 134
   Be attuned to where and with whom
     you are interacting 135
   Celebrating together 138
   Reasons to ignore cultural variance 140

IV. **Distinctive Places and Sites** 147

9. Getting Paid
   How not to accept 18 gross of native
   straw baskets (a true story) 149

   Round up the usual suspects (normal obstacles) 149
   Terms of endearment (how to grease the skids) 152
   Expenses are expensive 156
   The express lane 160

10. The Human Software for Global Consulting
    How to make the continuing sale to yourself 165

    Making the ongoing sale: Self-esteem 166
    Enthusiasm for the ongoing sale: Pick your friends 170
    Opportunities for the ongoing sale: Pick your clients 174
    Calibrating the ongoing sale: Choose your feedback 174
    Progress is what matters 177

11. Life Balance
   Enjoying the challenge   179

   Time balance   180
   Family and emotional balance   184
   Mental balance   188
   Energy balance   191
   Making a life   194

Appendices   197

   A. Best Ways to Travel   197

   Planes   197
   Trains   198
   Water travel   199
   Other noteworthy travel modes   199

   B. Our Favorite Hotels and Restaurants
      in Some of Our Favorite Cities   201

   New York   201
   London   202
   Paris   204
   Istanbul   205
   Dubai   205
   Bangkok   206
   Singapore   206
   Hong Kong   207
   Shanghai   208
   Tokyo   208
   Australia   209
   Others   210

   C. Vacation Glory   213

   Omar   213
   Alan   216

   Index   219

We dedicate this book with love and appreciation to Maria and Leslie, who have enabled and shared our travels, creating wonderful memories and beautiful futures.

Acknowledgments

We want to thank our clients who have provided the reason, means, and wealth that have enabled us to forge such wonderful international careers. We're proud to have provided them with value, and eternally indebted for the value they have provided us.

Introduction

We became global consultants by accident. That is, we didn't go to school and major in consulting, nor did we eventually enter into consulting with the clear strategy that "global" was key to our success.

We were simply both flexible enough ("wise" would appear to be too grandiose, in retrospect) to realize quickly that if the world wasn't flat, it was at least *accessible,* and the more buyers, the better! And that was in a day before cell phones, laptops, PDAs, webinars, and luxury travel to virtually every world nook and cranny. It was a day when Air Egypt, as you'll read later in this book, was the logical alternative between Tokyo and Manila.

The appeal of working across borders includes personal growth, enriched lives, and the opportunity to share with loved ones. Having said that, it had better be financially lucrative, so our subtitle is intended to convey the essence of our argument: You can and should be making seven figures in consulting through these peregrinations. By all means, build in vacation, recreation, and accommodation. But you'd better also be building financial security and net worth.

Our intent is to take you from the rudiments of travel essentials, marketing challenges, cultural adaptation, and self-education, right through the sophistication of collecting payments, working remotely, and international luxuries. That's because we fully expect that you may have to begin with the former, but you'll wind up with the latter if you take us seriously.

Only you control your talent and discipline. But you can learn the process and content of global consulting from our experiences, techniques, and the skills we transfer in this book.

If you're serious about consulting, you can't afford to ignore the world village. And if you're serious about global consulting, you can't afford to ignore our prescriptions and advice.

We've been there and done it, and continue to do so. We're not the ski instructors in the chalet sipping brandy and spouting advice. We're in front of you on the black diamond hill, demonstrating what you should do.

Just follow us, to a world of wealth.

— **Alan Weiss**
East Greenwich, RI
September 2008

— **Omar Khan**
New York, NY
September 2008

Part I

The Worldview

Chapter 1

Why Go Global?

*Because it's as easy to consult in
Kuala Lumpur as it is in Kansas*

In 1994, Alan Weiss traveled 174,000 miles by air, which was almost 75 percent of the time. In 2007, he traveled 37,000 miles—a record low *since 1972*—which accounted for about 15 percent of his time. He made twice as much in 2007 as he did in 1994.

In 1994, Omar Khan worked about 300 days a year and rarely could take time off. He was a prisoner of various markets. In 2007, he took five substantial vacations, did one-third of the physical delivery, and earned well over double what he did in 1994.

Are you starting to get the picture?

We hear a lot about Tom Friedman's *Flat Earth* and global competition and arising markets. But the fact is that innovative merchants and traders have followed global routes since antiquity, from the spice traders to the silk merchants to the navigators offering their services. People from the English court wound up in St. Petersburg, and rare metals from the Malay peninsula were transshipped to Spain, while English shipbuilding was exported to America, Africa, and the Far East.

Business people have always "gone global." It's simply easier now, because you can place a service on the Internet, rather than your backside on a camel. The alternatives have changed, but the objective has always been the same: Search out new and lucrative markets.

The earth isn't flat, it's right here

So now that we've quickly established that this isn't a new phenomenon, and with apologies to the learned Mr. Friedman, we'd like to suggest that the worldwide market is all around us. Let's start with the obvious.

As much as we adore camels, the Internet has created a seamless global interface. It is far, far more than mere information exchange. Customers talk to customers, vendors to vendors, prospects to prospects, even competitors to competitors. There is a huge knowledge base, augmented and catalyzed by social networking phenomena, which transcends the "mere" technological.

There is a website maintained and sustained by consumers, for example, called "citibanksucks.com" (<http://citibanksucks.com/>), and you can guess what kind of knowledge is being exchanged about that organization. At My3Cents.com (<www.my3cents.com/search.cgi?criteria=UPS>), you can learn all the ways in which, for example, United Parcel Service has ticked off, annoyed, and otherwise alienated its customers—globally. You can do the same for scores of industries and top companies.

We want to emphasize that this global tropism is not of recent vintage. It is simply exacerbated and turbocharged by existing and developing technology. While people today complain that "big box" stores such as Wal-Mart or Home Depot drive out small retailers, the truth is that the first long-distance railroads brought the sales power of Sears Roebuck through its print catalogs to rural areas, displacing, you guessed it, small stores.

Just as Marco Polo brought the Orient to the West, and the Union Pacific brought home appliances to the plains, the Internet is bringing knowledge to the world. Kuala Lumpur is where it always was (although fewer than 20 percent of Americans, at least, could probably find it), but the *consumer* in K.L. is now a keystroke away.

Closer than next door, if you get our drift. The Internet makes the stereotypical "Avon lady" or Fuller Brush salesman seem like a rugged road warrior by comparison.

Thus the world market for consulting services today is a matter more of perspective, not geography. That's not controlled in Asia, Europe, your own home, or even on your keyboard.

It's controlled between your ears.

If you believe you have a global market and global appeal, those values will inform your behavior. If you believe that "global" means "foreign" or "alien," then that philosophy will influence your behavior. These are worldwide cultural norms.

For example, in working with Canadian professional service providers in consulting, speaking, training, facilitating, and the like, we've found that the great preponderance do not feel that they can go "south" to the largest economic engine in history. The U.S., at this writing, is a US$14 trillion economy, and it sits just a few miles south of the narrow strip on which most of the 30 million Canadians live, and 90 percent of its professional service providers.

Yet we're told that there are language problems, problems of origin, visa problems, green card problems, travel problems, and all kinds of other problems. Then we point out two simple facts, not problems, facts:

- Both of us are doing business in Canada easily, although we are not citizens.
- We know a dozen Canadians doing a lot of business cross-border in the U.S.

How can those facts be so with those "problems" extant?

Simple: What you believe colors your behavior. The Europeans believed they could create a cross-border system without immigration and economic restrictions, and have been pretty successful in so doing. While there are companies like the German Hochtief (the top construction company in Germany) operating on key projects in the U.K., in a more general sense, it will probably be a long time before there is a truly seamless flow of such services across the borders, particularly for public works jobs. But we coach consultants all the time who are busy and successful pan-Europe.

The "knowledge business" is much easier to export!

Even if we do it the hard way, global work is easier than you think. In other words, it requires about six hours to travel from New York to Los Angeles, which is only an hour or two less than it takes to go the other way and travel to London or Paris, from London or Paris to Dubai, from Dubai to Singapore, and from Singapore to Sydney. You can circumnavigate the globe in small "jumps" if you desire, with no more trouble than a transcontinental trip within the U.S. Immigration adds 40 minutes, not 40 days.

So whether you travel by plane or browser, the world is nearby, virtually *and* physically.

Having said that, let's make it clear that physical travel is very important. That's because the Internet, fax, phone, and mail can never really replicate the experience of wandering around in a packed Tokyo subway, eating fish and chips in London[1], seeing the Outback in Australia, or hitting the beach in Key West, Florida. To be successful globally, you have to be a "globalist," and that means first-hand experiences. While it's true that Prince Henry, popularly known as the "The Navigator," never left Portugal, you can excuse him for demurring on a six-month experiment when his captains could keep him informed. But we can't excuse you from that six-hour plane trip we noted.

Global learning

You can intellectually learn about other parts of the world, but you must emotionally experience them to become a sophisticated cross-border consultant.

When we return from our travels, we tend to see things with fresh perspective, with prejudices removed and a more sympathetic mind and heart. We're actually more effective with local clients, in addition to the remote ones.

Travel nourishes the soul.

Physically and virtually, the world is not remote, not "flat," not around the corner, not next door. It's here.

All around you.

We are more alike than apart

There is an old anecdote in the consulting profession about two consultants assigned to sell footwear on opposite coasts of Africa. One cables back and says, "Send passage home, no one here wears shoes." The other cables back, "Send reinforcements, no one here wears shoes!"

That kind of disparity has the same impact for all of us, in that it's our perception and inventiveness that count. Peter Drucker commented continually that knowledge and expertise exports ought to be counted in the balance of trade. Countries worry about "brain drain" today, and whether people are fleeing China for Canada, France for the U.S., or Sweden for Norway.

Not long ago, sitting in a Sheraton hotel in Santiago, Chile, we found our hosts speaking fluent English, the newspaper store selling the *Miami Herald*, the cocktail hostess taking drink orders in English, and the band in the lounge playing Cole Porter. On that same trip, in Miami, we were eagerly practicing our Spanish on our hosts in that city, while listening to Cuban music, and smoking cigars from Nicaragua.

Wander into a Whole Foods Market, and if you emerge with the wherewithal for a superb dinner, it is likely that you will have taken a world tour with produce and condiments, meat or fish, possibly wine and cheese, coffee, and chocolates, that hail from numerous international ports.

Travel the world (which is assumed in this book's premise) and you'll find human challenges, opportunities, barriers, processes, foibles, emotions, passions, and aspirations that could be transported to thousands of different physical localities and not change one whit. This is not to deny cultural variation, but those variations are more social and superficial whereas the human and business needs are more deep seated and vital.

Australian colleagues often half-joke that they are ten years behind the U.S., for example, in adapting certain business practices. Yet they say the time differential used to be 20 years, and is closing.

Knowledge is knowledge and value is value. The importance of improved productivity, reduced cost, insightful strategy, and innovative leadership are transnational, cross-border constants. Only in a completely socialist state would these be unimportant, and those outposts have become shockingly rare these days.

What we've discovered around the world are these positive consulting commonalities and negative consulting commonalities:

Positives

- Clear buyers who have interest in business outcomes and value. These are people who can provide you with payment, or "economic buyers."[2]
- Competitive needs in terms of market share, labor costs, consumer loyalty, profit margins, and so forth.
- Preference for expertise over proximity, and credentials over nationality. Companies seeking to grow are passionately nonxenophobic.
- Innovative mindsets which embrace the proposition that "fixing" is insufficient, and that "raising the bar" is the way to stand out in a competitive universe.

- Intelligent uses of technology to overcome time and space differences and increase continual learning.

Negatives

- Consultants who charge by the hour or time unit, positioning themselves as competitive commodities.
- A focus on deliverables; that is, input over output. (The training session instead of the increase in sales.)
- Packaged and precooked interventions that are superimposed on clients, instead of customized and tailored approaches created specifically for the client's culture and needs.
- Excessive labor intensity, travel, and attendant expenses for the client.
- Poor use of technology and media to exploit strengths.

Are you getting the picture? The positives are that there is a great market awaiting consulting help. The negatives are that the consultants laboring around the world mostly don't "get" it. They are positioned wrongly, delivering wrongly, and charging wrongly.

So there is a great opportunity and it is a great time to be a cross-border consultant. No one cares where you're from. The probability is that you can do better than those who are already there.

Global learning

Clients are not all that interested in people who look like them, and certainly not in people who think like them. They crave someone with a fresh viewpoint.

There isn't only a basic human nature at work here, there is a basic business nature. Capitalism has won the global battle of dominant economic systems, and for all its imperfections, it looks as though it's here to stay. While part of the attraction is the booming economy in Norway due to their natural resources, specifically oil, people have been leaving Sweden in droves looking for such opportunities because of local economic stagnation and deadening social welfare constraints (speeding fines are also adjusted based on your income!).

Sweden was neutral in World War II, and gained the advantage of sustaining no major damage to its manufacturing and production infrastructure. It accelerated rapidly post-war, while others were rebuilding under the Marshall Plan.

Today, however, that old advantage has been wiped out through a lack of reward for internal innovation and risk (and consequent income growth). Excellent health systems and schools are wonderful, but alone are not sufficient to keep and nurture talent, which requires challenge and growth. Consequently, people look to Norway, where oil resources are creating dynamic job growth.

These are realities, not chauvinism or projections or isolated events:

- Technology has effectively shifted time, so that we can all correspond and communicate from wherever we are (mobile phones) whenever we like (email awaiting us) with whatever impact makes sense (text, graphics, voice, animation, and so forth).
- English has become a standard language. Not only do all air traffic controllers use it, but almost all high-level executives in international firms must. In Germany, as an example, there are firms comprising German managers in which English is the spoken language.
- Monetary transfer is easy. Credit cards, wire transfers, overseas accounts, and other alternatives make it simple to charge and collect fees rapidly.

We'll focus more on this in the next section. We introduce it here because these are factors accentuating our increasing "alikeness" and decreasing "apartness." Today, we see call centers in Bangalore providing responses to American consumers; Brazilian jets (Embraer) being sold to airlines around the world; the Chinese hosting the Olympics and concerned about environmental pollution; Russians making deals to supply much of Europe with oil and gas; and the U.S. and Mexico struggling with millions—*millions*—of illegal transnationals, who are working, getting paid, paying taxes, and using the infrastructure.

Tribalism and ethnic identities still pose problems, but they are restricted to zealots and fanatics, and are almost always in places in which capitalism is not employed or has not been embraced, from Northern Ireland to Iran, from Burma to North Korea.

Those are the exceptions. Let's address the rule.

Harsh truth: American English, American dollars, American knowledge

We have been careful to prepare and write this book with a truly global, not merely multinational, approach. However, we must face this fact early and candidly before we delve into later strategies and tactics: This has become an American-influenced business world.

One of us was born in Egypt while being originally a Pakistani national (that seeming oddity due to Omar's father being a career diplomat), and one in Hoboken, New Jersey. One of us resides full time in the U.S., and one maintains residence and citizenship here, while also globe-hopping and keeping apartments in Dubai and Paris. Yet both of us are true globalists and successful at it because we've come to acknowledge a simple fact about American business influence.

We've established the means to communicate rapidly and globally by using satellites, Internet, fax, phone, and so on. But the content of the communications must be common. The stories about Chinese villagers not being able to speak to the villagers over the next hill are quite true, and the dialects of China (and in pre-unified Italy or Germany centuries ago) prevented the rapid growth of internal trade. The most prized people in exploration Europe were those who could converse in French, Spanish, Arabic, and so on, permitting rapid trade agreements, safe passage, and signed treaties. The stories may or may not be apocryphal about English monarchs who couldn't speak English, but it is quite clear that the monarchy preferred to speak in its own, non-native tongue, and French was overwhelmingly the *lingua franca* of the day. The fact that they couldn't converse with their peasants and serfs was irrelevant.

For a variety of historic reasons and events that we needn't reiterate here, American English is the dominant means of communications cross-culturally. You couldn't run an air traffic system where pilots had to learn the language of the local air traffic controllers so that they could land. International banking and investment would be impossible. No matter what country one travels to, the immigration people will either speak some English, or have available someone who does; travel *to* the U.S. and you may find some Spanish speaking immigration people at major airports, but the likelihood is that you'd better speak some English if you want a smooth passage through the system.

We make no value judgment. We are merely stating facts.

In the nineteenth century, we would have counseled facility in British English and probably a working knowledge of French. Times change, and the U.S. rise to global dominance has coincided with a mass communication and mass technological revolution that have both been largely U.S. led.

Despite the euro (and the dollar's weakness at this writing, which is a cyclical event), the American dollar is the currency standard. Some Central and South American countries have experimented with using the dollar as their daily currency, actually do use it, or use it illegally in that manner without admitting it. (We can't remember the last time in that region we couldn't use American dollars no matter where we were, and certainly not in a major market.) The euro is doing quite well as we write this, as is the Canadian dollar. How do we know? Because they are judged against American currency, just as is the price of oil or gold.

Whether you are an American who takes this, unfortunately, for granted, or a non-American who has to grapple with a perceived inequity, this is the reality, and is it really so harsh?

After all, we welcomed the Japanese as the leaders in consumer electronics and quality control. What was once the "poor quality" of Japanese manufacturing after World War II has become the world standard for excellence, led by firms such as Toyota and Sony. (Of no small irony is that Dr. W. Edwards Deming, the quality guru, was ignored in his home country, the U.S., and made his mark stimulating quality in Japan, where he is a legendary figure.)

The French Michelin Guide is the gold standard for top culinary achievement. Milan and Paris have set fashion standards for decades. London, sitting on Greenwich Mean Time, continues as a financial center because its business hours coincide partly with both New York's and the major Asian markets. Many standards of marketing and trade develop for a confluence of reasons, and we must adapt to this inevitable dynamic, not bemoan it. In the U.S., students learning to speak, say, Japanese or Mandarin may well excel in business more than those who do not undertake that rigor, but it is still not correctly as critical as it is for a Japanese or Chinese student to learn English.

While "nation building" is generally abhorred (at least in politically correct conversation), American-style democracy and the reverence for free speech and press have traveled the globe with increasing receptivity. A strongman like Hugo Chavez in Venezuela can suffer a policy defeat at the polls. You can now name the repressive dictatorships using memory: Korea, Cuba, the Mideast theological monarchies, Burma, a few African strongmen, you get the idea..

It's common to see American clothing on kids in Ecuador, American television reruns in the U.K., and carbon copies of American news shows and anchors in Dubai or Delhi. CNN is a universal news station, and ESPN and MTV provide similar commonality for sports and pop culture.

Global learning

There is a growing acceptance of the universality of news, sports, and management thought leadership.

Centers for excellence—or for fads and trends and crazes—emerge from every culture that has had a strong economic history. For our purposes, the most important point for consultants working cross-border is that the U.S. has forged universal thought leadership in so many areas, particularly in management, strategy, and business leadership.

There are, of course, great thinkers in these areas all over the globe, and fine institutions, such as INSEAD in Switzerland. But the sheer influence and volume emanating from the U.S. is unparalleled. Peter Drucker maintained that if you created financial worth around the export of business knowledge—which he thought eminently feasible—that America would have a positive balance of trade and erase the deficit if we included the results. (Interestingly, he included the worth of foreign students studying at U.S. institutions of higher learning in these calculations. The University of Tokyo is a wonderful place, and *the* only place to go if you want to reach the top tier in Japanese business and society. But other nationalities can't and won't go there. They do come to the U.S., where many institutions can lead you to the "top tier," and you can see this diversity at virtually any American college campus.)[3]

In Australia, they often called Americans "wise men from the East." Our own experience is that at the height of anti-American political sentiments in any one place at any one time, major businesses were still aggressively seeking American management help.

Speaking in South America two years ago, we were astounded to find that the local promoters would fill a convention center hall with 250 people at US$1,000 per seat for one day of Alan Weiss speaking on selling mastery, and one day of a professor from the Kellogg School at Northwestern speaking about competitive dynamics. This occurred through five cities, and bear in mind that the average income in Chile, for example, was US$12,000, and in Ecuador, US$6,000 per year.

The U.K., which has many fine institutions and many fine thinkers in the field of management and leadership, nevertheless has arguably contributed only one major guru by global standards—Charles Handy. In London, a center of global standards and taste in many arenas, Alan's recent session, "The Strategist," played to a sold-out crowd. Omar, touted there as an American, booked in 2007 400,000 British pounds (as of this writing about US$800,000) of consulting business without living there or having an office on the ground, and many U.S. provocateurs like Tom Peters, who rant with American-style embellishments, are sought after and booked there annually.

This week, the Korean version of *Million Dollar Consulting* was published, joining its "colleagues" of 25 other books appearing in eight languages. One of the first translations of *Money Talks,* a book about professional speaking, was, amazingly, in long-form Chinese (as was *Getting Started in Consulting*).

Combining the rush to global markets with sophisticated immediacy in communications and the long-standing dominance of American English, dollars, and culture, the short-term future of cross-border consulting is in exploiting, not fighting, these realities. That's because capitalism does not depend on government, nationality, or ethnicity.

Capitalism compels collaboration

One of the most powerful reasons to consult across borders is that capitalism, for all its flaws, has defeated the other pretenders to the throne of economic success. Capitalism is the Esperanto of economics.

By that, we mean that capitalism favors no language, product, service, market, or demographic, except successful ones. It is based on a Judeo-Christian value of ethical conduct. Yet the Chinese are now also tapping their pragmatic Confucian roots to pursue what is essentially capitalism under the guise of "communism," and Muslim traders in the heydays of that civilization also conducted themselves in accordance with similar principles. In other words, you promise to provide a certain product or service at a certain time in a certain place of a certain quality or duration, and I promise to provide a certain remuneration of a certain amount in a certain form for a certain period time. Capitalism is based on trust. If the trust is routinely violated, the system collapses. More importantly, those who violate the trust find themselves disenfranchised from the system.[4]

Global learning

You can create your own "international team" by using people on the ground in various locations who are eager to deliver and nurture what you sell and create.

On a more micro level, we find that there are relatively few rainmakers but hordes of delivery people. Transnationally, there are tens of thousands of "consultants" and "trainers" and "facilitators" and "coaches" who love their methodology and rejoice in delivering projects, *but cannot market or sell.* Consequently, the capitalist tropism creates a natural blend of collaboration for those who can make rain (create business) and those who can harvest (deliver and maintain business).

These contacts are relatively easy to find and develop through the Internet, international professional associations, existing colleagues, and word of mouth. If we needed resources in Hong Kong, Milan, Sydney, or Dubai, we could be in discussions in a matter of hours, and have a deal in place in a day.

The advantage to the individuals who perform the delivery include:

- becoming part of an international network
- guaranteed work
- learning from you
- exposure to new clients and new markets
- increased personal branding

The advantages to you in this relationship include:

- international "presence"
- cultural synergy

- language compatibility
- faster local responsiveness
- client development for repeat business
- local lead generation

Naturally, this is based on finding people you can trust and who do excellent work, but our experience is that this is rather easy using the technique outlined. So long as it is "win/win/win" (client/subcontractor/you) then the power of capitalism will maintain and nourish the relationship.

We want to make clear that these are pragmatic, tangible projects and collaborations. Whether the other party is a subcontractor merely following your instructions, or an alliance partner equally engaged with you, money and business are on the table.

Conceptual collaborations are almost always a huge waste of time and energy. Theoretical alliances virtually never culminate in business, but they require inordinate time and energy to plan, discuss, design, and so on. We can theoretically combine lion tamers and nutritionists, or do team-building experiences with dentistry. Who cares? It's never going to actually happen, no matter how elaborate and perfect the diagrams and PowerPoint slides.

Bear in mind, also, the difference between a subcontractor and an alliance partner.

Subcontractor

This is a person who delivers on your behalf. That may be workshops, interviews, focus groups, assessments, whatever. They are normally paid per diem or hourly. They should *never* have a "piece of the action," because they are easy to find and need you, because if they could market themselves, they wouldn't be subcontracting for delivery! Never pay for anything more than performance, and have strict contracts about what they can and cannot do on your behalf.

Alliance partners

These are people or firms who bring business to the table. You may jointly deliver, or even have subcontractors deliver. They are very useful when acquisition partners of local origin are keys to acquiring business, or when language is an issue. (Sometimes, legally, you must have a local partner, as well.) In these cases, fees and expenses are shared according to who brings in the business, whose methodology is used, and who delivers the project.

We'll talk more about these relationships in the chapters to come. We merely wanted to establish to this point that global consulting is not restricted by borders, regulations, technology, language, origins, or any other external factor.

Rather, it is increased by your vantage point, vision, and volition to be a global consultant.

World tour

- Knowledge is valuable and prized from any source.

- The commonalities far outweigh separateness.

- The key commonalities are language, money, culture, and capitalism.

- You can establish global resources and local people "on the ground."

- Technology is the great time shifter.

Endnotes

1. At today's rates, fish and chips, once a staple, are starting to look like a delicacy!
2. Alan Weiss has pioneered the concepts of seeking out economic buyers and selling value, not "deliverables." For the best synopsis in one place, see *Million Dollar Consulting* (McGraw-Hill, third edition: 2002), and for guideline for how to enter this mindset, see *Getting Started in Consulting* (Wiley, third edition: 2008).
3. It is no small irony that American primary and secondary education is so woeful in the public sector, but its universities are so excellent, diverse, and widely available.
4. This is why global business in corrupt states is never a good idea. If the "ethic" is to try to cheat the other party, then there is no "win/win" dynamic, and criminality prevails.

Chapter 2

Projecting Expertise and Building Relationships

How to be nearby from 8,000 miles away

One of the biggest mental barriers to global consulting (most of the truly crippling barriers to *anything* originate with our limiting thoughts and paradigms) is the fear that we can't project our expertise half a world away. Moreover, we wonder how we can compete with those who are actually physically present in these distant markets?

The answer: Fairly readily if you build a true brand, and base your practice on intellectual capital and value, rather than labor intensity.

There are many ways to produce a true sense of "being there," even if you are actually counting grains of sand on your favorite beach in Cancun with a pomegranate margarita at the time. There are also ways that technology and the right relationships can allow you to reach out or stay connected at critical moments. Finally, there are ways of maximizing your impact when you do travel, so that your key economic buyers deeply experience value and savor the trusting relationship you've established with them long after you've headed home.

The trick to projecting expertise: First get the right type

The right type of expertise, almost by definition, isn't a commodity, and therefore isn't readily on tap locally in a way that then seems both more cost effective and convenient than you can provide.

So if you position your consulting practice as running team-building programs, you'll run into a problem. Essentially, any local adventure company with even modest facilitation skills can cobble together a few days, based on interactive exercises that allow them to then debrief on aspects of building a team.

You may argue that your exercises are better: your program design is scintillating, your delivery far more inspired, and your experience in working with teams deeper and more relevant. Fine, let's even concede you're correct in your assessment.

The problem is that at a distance, all you can do is assert it. For your potential client to believe you, they have to buy into you to experience it—which is then precisely the Catch-22 problem with this type of generic positioning.

However, if your expertise was more focused, and your positioning included (for example) that you help diverse global groups to become a real team to produce a true, specified business result; and you had a brand and client references that substantiated this claim, then no vendor of common team games or abstruse outdoor antics could have a similar conversation with your clients, no matter where they were living.

Omar was asked to conduct a leadership journey in the Philippines. This involves taking a leadership team on a physical journey through a distinctive locale, and having pivotal business conversations along the way. It is a distinctive value offering, which helps them bond, experience a new culture, expand paradigms, and in the process of doing so, have key conversations that can make a true difference to their business. (If you're interested in seeing how this fleshes out, visit <www.sensei-international.com>, and under "How We Can Help," visit "Leadership Quest.")

To put on the journey for his client, Omar was introduced by the client to a local adventure and team-building company for logistics support. This company played a secondary support role, and there certainly was no issue of it supplanting Omar and his team, despite being locally present, because the leadership journey brand and expertise sought by the client were utterly distinctive.

Similarly, around the world, if you were to try and enter a market by saying you have a "presentation skills" course, you would render people catatonic. Everyone from local Toastmasters to Dale Carnegie offices, to countless local trainers, works in this value space. Yet be able to credibly say that you help leaders refine their message, find their own personal voice, and express themselves confidently and powerfully so that they move their listeners to action, and you've got a business-furthering dialog on your hands.

Alan routinely sells out proprietary, high-end, single-day sessions on strategy, or coaching, or fee setting from halfway around the world. That's because they have gained publicity by selling out in the U.S., and this might be the "only chance to participate" in far-flung locations (at least, "far flung" for Alan!).

So, in short, the right expertise travels. It travels because common problems abound whenever human dynamics are involved, and they transcend cultural differences. How to improve customer loyalty amid a plethora of competing leisure options is as much of a challenge for the luxury Aman Resorts Hotel Chain in the old Fort Town of Galle, Sri Lanka as it is for their Jackson Hole Ski Property in Wyoming.

Global learning

When our brand is powerful enough and our niche is valuable enough, geography fades as a consideration; and people seek us out gladly and eagerly.

So we need a distinctive "edge," an approach that our brand communicates that translates readily into palpable value for buyers. It behooves us to communicate that expansively and distinctively, not in terms of methodologies, toolkits, or programs that are always teetering at or near their "sell by" date as the next "in" thing is being minted somewhere else. No matter the fads, in the meantime, serious organizations and leaders will continue to need real work to be done on behalf of results they're answerable for. Let's make sure we're focusing there.

For example, Alan doesn't mentor people in "coaching certifications," some nifty new behavioral technology, or a glitzy prepackaged sales system. However, his ability to use common sense insightfully and pragmatically, backed by years of actual experience with discerning clients around the world, allows him to have an approach that others can learn from, readily deploy, and thereby reap measurable results. That's not something likely to fade!

Breaking in is relatively easy to do

The next question is, with some branded and distinctive expertise in hand, how do I actually enter various global markets?
Some of it will happen naturally from brand-building efforts.
For example, as you have commercially published books, articles
in major magazines, a website that draws traffic from those who
are interested in your subject area; as you give talks that have in
the audience people who may refer you to colleagues overseas or
companies with many global operating bases, you will begin to
get more than cursory nibbles of interest.

But we are assuming here that you want to expand your markets actively, expand your brand overseas deliberately, and reap
the profits and stimulus of consulting more globally.
That being the case, you can guide latent interest and perhaps
even help arouse it in many ways.

More than anything, pick markets that attract you—culturally,
historically, economically, and otherwise. Decide where you'd
like to travel to, what you'd like to experience, and then take aim
accordingly.

A Canadian sales expert, Bob Urichuck, wanted to take his
speaking and consulting work outside of North America. His
approach was classic Sales 101. He wrote letters to every hotel
in Singapore (regional Asian hub with a high degree of economic wellbeing, many multinationals, and so on), offering to
run a free half-day session on sales and service for their employees in return for a free stay in a suite for a week.

The Holiday Inn Crowne Plaza said "yes," and Bob booked
introductory talks at the Singapore Institute of Management, got
introductions from North American clients to their counterparts
in Asia, offered to speak at the American Chamber of
Commerce, and filled a week with appointments that had a high
likelihood of being productive.

He was in his early 40s when he did this. Less than a decade
later, he had a thriving business in terms of consulting, presentations, and product sales in Singapore, Dubai, Australia, and
elsewhere. Thanks to this global expansion, he was also able to
"retire" at 50, in the sense of having built and paid off his dream
house in Canada, having funded the education of his kids, and

having safely invested enough money for his wife and him to retire on. However, he continues to use the global work as a vehicle for seeing the world, earning, and having fun.

Bob's chutzpah in aggressively contacting people and establishing his bona fides, and thereby establishing a beachhead may seem extreme, but all of us can repeat the ingredients.

Find good local institutes in places you wish to do business, gather introductions from clients at home, offer to give speeches at notable conferences, let prominent bookstores know you'll be in town and offer to do a book signing, or contact eminent journals and send in an article or offer an interview.

Additionally, while all of these stratagems work and in short order can help you make inroads into chosen markets, let's not discount the serendipitous openings that come our way through simply using our interests and keeping our antennae up.

Years back, Omar delivered a conference for American Express in Colombo, Sri Lanka (interestingly nicknamed "Serendip" relating to an ancient Persian fable "The Three Princes of Serendip," from which British writer and essayist Horace Walpole was to pluck the word "serendipity"—literally meaning *sagacity in the face of good fortune* not just "good luck"). Sri Lanka is a beautiful if tragic land. Happily, at the time Omar went for the Conference, its civil war was in abeyance, and the country was enjoying a period of relative calm and prosperity.

At the conference, Omar's speech attracted the attention of the general manager of the Hilton in Colombo, Gamini Fernando. He was interested in part due to Omar's experience working with The Ritz-Carlton hotel group, which at that time, was the standard setter in the hotel industry. As a result, Omar returned to Colombo several times for work with the Hilton and other clients.

Gamini managed to attract the global wining and dining society, the Chaine des Rotisseurs to Colombo. This was quite a coup for Colombo.

On a Chaine trip in Italy with Gamini, Omar promised that he and his wife, Leslie, would host the next Chaine event in Dubai, where they also had by this time many clients and an operating base. The Sri Lankan members were keen to experience this increasingly famous emirate.

One of the attendees was the chairman of Unilever in Sri Lanka. He was known as a demanding taskmaster. He loved the wine and food and arrangements, and corralled Omar one evening by the pool. "I've been overwhelmed by how well put together this is. What do you do for a living, by the way?"

This conversation led to Omar's first consulting job for Unilever. Seven years later, Unilever is one of the largest global clients for Omar's firm, Sensei, and has done US$300,000 to half a million dollars of business minimum with Omar each year since then. Serendipity indeed!

Global learning

Use a combination of market-opening tactics and being alert enough to respond creatively when opportunity knocks.

Omar's work with and interest in hotels originally led to his working with the Ritz-Carlton. While in Sri Lanka, this gave Omar a basis for igniting a relationship with Hilton International and Gamini. Working with Gamini in turn led to being invited to participate in events hosted by the Sri Lanka Chaine des Rotisseurs. Then, when he and Leslie designed and hosted a visit for the Chaine to Dubai, this allowed an exacting global client to see them in action, so to speak. And that has produced millions of dollars of consulting income with that client, all the way from Sri Lanka to Egypt to Morocco to Vietnam, to Thailand, to Singapore, to Hong Kong, to England, and more.

Once you've got the relationships, keep connecting

The aim is to create virtual presence. This is done in a variety of ways. There are first active ways such as email offerings, teleconferences, in-person- and e-seminars, new books or CDs, newsletters, and various other forms of offered benefit.

As people respond to these and benefit from them, they will naturally visit your website, which can be further replete with everything from articles, blogs, podcasts, interviews, video clips, and more.

As people come to enjoy your "voice," your point of view, your perspective, your experiences, your take on life and business, they will gravitate to your various offerings.

As long as there are frequent updates and abundant value to be found, for example, in Alan's case with his topical *The Writing on the Wall* series and blog entries, in Omar's case with the "Insight of the Month" and frequent podcasts from various interviews, people then feel they are in dialogue with you. As they understand what you've been thinking and feeling and saying, they hardly feel you are "far away." They may even have more meaningful insight into the evolution of your perspectives, philosophies, passions, and ideas than they do of the people right next door.

So once you have an established relationship with clients, reach out to them with things that capture their attention, and give them enough value so that they are drawn to your website or your next appearance seeking "more." Their own thoughts and feelings will then confirm your *presence*.

Global learning

Through judicious direct and indirect contact, we can help people be more "in touch" with us than they are with people literally around the corner.

Moreover, you can then create a community of your clients and help put them together. Many of those mentored by Alan, for example, attend "Mentor Summits." Many people attend Alan's new workshops, like the globally successful "The Strategist," and comment on what a community of top-notch consultants Alan has nurtured.

If your consulting practice is currently more corporate based, you can do this too. Omar created a "best practice club" for his company's top clients, so they could interact with, challenge, and learn from each other. Each group had to be made up of noncompetitors, and even between the quarterly get-togethers, while Omar was away, they stayed in touch and built relationships—and the "club" kept Omar and his company Sensei in mind as they did so.

Another form of connectivity is through associates. As your brand gets known, some people will be happy to implement on your behalf. One of the best sources of such associates are smaller single-person consultancies or trainers. You will often see by their literature when they are methodology based, rather than brand or expertise based.

Find those who excel in companion methodologies or in overlapping areas of execution, and write a straightforward subcontractor's agreement with them. Ensure ideally that these are people you would enjoy working with and are good "representatives" as well. That way, if someone drops you an email from Auckland saying, "I'd love to have someone from your side present at a meeting about how we stop our projects from being chronically late and over budget," and you have a local associate colleague who you know has particular expertise relative to project work, you can get him or her over there, and agree the questions he or she is going to ask and the facts he or she is going to bring back to you, so that you and your economic buyer can discuss a way forward.

On the other hand, if you have ongoing clients in a location who are going to need to call, send documents over, or even stop by to see you or your associates from time to time, then you can consider arranging shared executive offices. In this regard, Regus and Landmark are well-known international brands, but each market has its own.

These usually will provide you a legal physical address, a dedicated phone line with someone who answers on behalf of your company, voicemail and message service, mail and basic admin, and conference rooms you can book as needed. The costs are not very much more than US$150 a month, scaling up based on what you need. However, it's a fast and convenient way to create presence, not only virtually but actually. We emphasize that even this much is often not needed. We each do business in countless locations where we have no such physical presence. However, if needed or helpful to the type of business or the type of contracts you have, this can be easily and affordably set up.

Chapter 3 has more details about the pros and cons of physical presence and offices.

As much as anything, both Alan and Omar, by also responding to calls and emails fast, within a known band of time, allow clients to feel that they can be in touch virtually whenever they want. That way, distance truly is illusory, because contactability, not whether you're spotted parked across the road, is what matters to clients.

Within the U.S., you can set up a 90-minute response commitment as Alan does to calls and agree to answer all emails the same day. Within 24 hours is still a commitment you can offer globally for emails, and on a regular basis, that's all that's needed. If you, as

Omar does when in New York, set up an 8:30 a.m. to 10:30 a.m. window for calls, virtually anybody can call you from around the world, knowing those are global "office hours" for you.

Amplifying the impact of your brand and presence: Adapting to local needs

It helps in seeking to provide global consulting if some of your examples are drawn from a wider pool of experience than your own zip code. That said, if you truly provide compelling value, as we've argued, you'll find human issues to be astonishingly common around the globe.

Yet even then, bridging from your universal points to people's particular issues magnifies the value of your brand and increases its attractiveness. There are simple ways to get a feel for the markets you wish to spend consulting time in.

Some years ago, veteran presenter and best-selling author Harvey Mackay was asked to address a major conference in Singapore. He asked to speak to a highly regarded regional speaker who would be participating. This regional speaker was delighted to have an opportunity to "coach" Harvey Mackay. In two hours, Harvey got a sense of the market, the crowd, the country, the mores, hot topics, areas of sensitivity, and more. How much of that made it into his 45-minute keynote? Perhaps not a lot. But he scored a real victory with that delighted crowd as he continued to allude to and refer to things that they recognized and that made his points highly relevant as well as generally insightful.

We contrast this with the crowd-numbing impact produced by one of the world's great strategy gurus, who came to the Middle East charging US$150,000 for a one-day presentation to a packed house. When asked in the Q&A how he would apply the precept he had been extolling to markets in the Middle East, he replied, "I don't have any idea, I don't know this place at all." He then continued undeterred by the spreading disaffection among a crowd that felt that US$150,000 didn't even earn it enough interest for him to have opened the morning paper before striding out on to the podium. It was a disaster, and he's unofficially "banned" in power circles in the region now—the very circles that are his primary consulting base.

If you're located in the U.S. or the U.K. or Hong Kong, you don't just "show up" in Cape Town or Buenos Aires as though you've caught a train to the next town down the line.

The mention of the paper isn't trivial. It's natural to be interested in where you're going—particularly if you think you may wish to return, establish a presence, generate a following, and earn significant profits.

It helps to build in some time to see the place, to get a feel for it. Chat with people in the hotel bar. Pick up the local papers. If there are interesting local authors, dip into their works. Watch a local TV channel for a while just to get a sense of the tempo. Walk the streets, take in interactions, pick up the vibe, and gain your own "feel" for the place.

Global learning

The better you understand the environment you are in, the more your imagination and distinctiveness can shine even in a "foreign" setting.

These types of exposure allow you, when you're not there, through allusions, or references, or examples, or by asking intelligent interested questions, to connect quickly with people in that location, and show you are genuinely interested in them as more than an ATM.

Omar was asked to do some work in Ireland recently for a county learning organization. He had a three-hour ride to his hotel, the stunning Ashford Castle on the shores of Lough Corrib, a beautifully restored thirteenth century castle that was once the estate of the Guinness family. His chauffeur had the Irish gift of gab, and was an engaging raconteur. By the end of the three hours, they had ranged through Irish politics, religion, folk bands and troubadours, challenges facing County Mayo, some of the personalities Omar would encounter, the character of Ashford Castle, and more.

Now the truth is that he started chatting once Omar engaged him, because he was well trained enough to have chauffeured in silence had Omar so chosen. But while neither of us is always up for a travelog, this was a new setting for Omar, and it was clear to him he had an unusually astute commentator on his hands. So as we said, keep the antennae up, and take advantage of all that you can.

That night at Ashford Castle, Omar also met the GM, who was a further treasure trove of insight, as well as cosseting Omar and Leslie with superb hospitality. By the time Omar met the leaders of the leadership council of County Mayo the next morning, he had not only been well versed in his surroundings, but *immersed*.

Did the work or content change substantially? No. They were asking for global input, not provincial reaffirmation, or Omar wouldn't have been there in the first place. But did the communication work better, were the examples more pertinent, did Omar understand their concerns better, was he able to connect in a way that was more meaningful to them, did they leave at the end with the basis of a relationship? Yes!

Omar's chauffeur–friend Eamonn said, "You can't believe the happy sheets [referring to the evaluation forms that both Alan and Omar believe to be largely a waste of time], you have to listen to the 'muttering' as they leave. You scored a real hit, my friend!" He seemed ready to break into an Irish jig with delight.

Alan has learned enough Spanish to talk conversationally to taxi drivers, restaurant servers, and bartenders, which enables him to quickly learn the local "scoop" that you may not read in the newspapers. He's also famous for chatting with people immediately before a meeting or speech, and using the most current of events to enliven his remarks, speech, or marketing presentation.

The other reason to be aware of local tastes, paradigms and viewpoints is that otherwise we import conclusions from our own backyard that the local audience may not share. Rather than promoting connectivity, this can cause unhelpful dissonance and distance.

For example, many of us look a tad warily at Singapore's politics, presided over as they largely are by a single party under the general oversight of Singapore's chief political architect, Lee Kuan Yew. Given that newspapers there are wise not to criticize the government openly and that the same party dominates after each election, we might well consider it somewhat authoritarian.

But don't tell that to proud, patriotic Singaporeans. What they see is that in a little more than 30 years, they've gone from being a war- and disease-riddled swamp under the shadow of other countries to being one of the most prosperous city-states and countries in the world. With a GDP at purchasing power parity per capita that is greater than that of Germany, and being an IT, banking, and services hub, the Lion City of Singapore has much to be proud of.

Answering critics, Lee Kuan Yew said that when governments have to run for office effectively every two to three years, they don't govern, they perennially pander for votes. On the other hand, he argued, governments with a longer mandate can build up their countries, and work on long-term problems such as education, competitiveness, health care, and more. Moreover, he is adamant that having a flourishing, diverse, multi-ethnic society provides for much freedom of expression, even if tight control is retained over anything that might, in the government's view, compromise law and order.

Reflecting on his views, we note that what works for a city-state and what works for a larger country or continent are very different things. Indeed, the first 40 years of independence in a region establishing democracy out of past chaos is a different challenge than that faced by mature democracies seeking to revitalize themselves.

This is worth mentioning only as an example of cherished local views to be aware of. Many of us may consider Malaysia's Mahathir Mohamad to have acted questionably when he jailed the progressive deputy prime minister, Anwar Ibrahim. To many Malaysians, Mahathir is a hero regardless. We don't have to agree. We need to be aware. There are debates we may wish not to enter, and viewpoints we need to at least understand, even if they aren't ones we are likely to embrace personally.

This is relevant because as we build relationships and spend social time, ideas will naturally be exchanged and points made, and strutting forth with our "view from the West" is unlikely to foster the mutual connection we are after. We can have spirited and stimulating dialogues, in which all kinds of views are batted around, but it helps to know the likely default positions in various societies on important areas of possible interest and concern—because we then have that as a launching pad.

Both Alan and Omar believe as lifelong contrarians that we don't have to pander to people, and our job is to be provocative, overseas no less than at home. But we both believe that is best done with some genuine insight, some knowledge of culture and history, and a willingness not only to stimulate others but to be stimulated ourselves. We don't believe everything we read in our own "home town" newspapers about the rest of the world. We validate and confirm.

One of the great attractions of global consulting is therefore that our own worldviews and perspectives expand, and that helps us not only "out there," but back home and in virtually everything we do. We learn more, we hopefully to some extent become capable of more—insight, awareness, creativity, and responsiveness.

World tour

- Have the kind of expertise that isn't a commodity, but is distinctive enough for people to seek you out.

- Offer "demos" in markets you wish to operate in.

- Let your interests and your networking lead you to profitable, if initially unplanned–for, opportunities.

- Use technology to create contact and buzz, to bring others together, and to allow them to interact with you from anywhere.

- Research facts, read local books and papers, talk to locals, experience the culture. Relevant adaptation then isn't an esoteric challenge, just good sense.

Creating International Presence

Alliances and the appeal of the knowledge exporter

As this chapter is written, the two of us have finished emailing each other between Dubai and Rhode Island. Between us, we have conducted business, this morning/afternoon (Rhode Island/Dubai) in Indonesia, Korea, the U.K., Saudi Arabia, Hong Kong, Singapore, Canada, and Australia. We've accomplished this through:

- email
- phone calls
- Internet interaction
- product sales
- teleconference
- local partners
- published articles and columns
- blog postings and responses

And one of us has just finished breakfast and the other a late lunch!

What Drucker said

The first thing you must internalize is that "presence" does not rely on physical proximity. That sounds like an oxymoron, but it's the warp and woof of global consulting. We all watched the British depart from Hong Kong in the rain, with a single bagpiper playing a morose tune as he walked into the mist, and, with him, British influence. We didn't have to be present for the poignancy of the moment, nor did we have to be amid the tanks in Tiananmen Square to appreciate the heroism of the man standing his ground in front of an iron behemoth representing the totalitarian power of the state.

There was a Super Bowl played in Arizona in 2008 in a stadium labeled and referred to as "Phoenix University." The rather interesting background is that the stadium doesn't belong to Phoenix University—which merely paid to have its name on the edifice and the advertising and promotion—because there is no physical "Phoenix University." It is a virtual institution of learning, conducting 100 percent of its coursework, tests, communications, and student interactions over the Internet. No one is housed, fed, or clothed there.

There is no "there."

Yet there is a university and students and degrees. Similarly, there is your expertise, transfer mechanisms, accessibility, results, and so on. But you needn't be "there," or anywhere in particular. One of the best selling of current business books remains *Think and Grow Rich* by Napoleon Hill. He is long since deceased, but his intellectual property continues. Knowledge takes on its own presence and meaning, apart from its originator and perpetrator.

Global learning

Your international presence can be physical, virtual, or a combination of both. It's up to you to choose your ratio. But don't allow your default position to be an airplane trip.

As we've noted, Peter Drucker, the inventor of modern strategy, long maintained that knowledge export is the most important and valuable of all exports. Universities all over the world have demonstrated this through extension courses, and Phoenix University has taken it to a new level by being completely virtual, except when it chooses, briefly, like a wraith in the night, to attach its name to something!

What Drucker said applies to you. We don't mean it might apply to you, or could apply to you. We mean that it *does* apply to you, and the real question is whether you intend to establish an international presence.

Here are some simple strategies to create local presence without being present. (Later in this chapter, we'll discuss local physical alliances and your own travel.)

Publish locally

We are constantly sought out by international sources to provide articles and columns in journals and periodicals. (India is quite thirsty for such input.) Usually, these are English-language publications, as supported in Chapter 1. But we've been asked, for example, by the largest German-language business magazine in Europe (located in Switzerland, by the way) to excerpt a book on strategy, and by the Catholic Church to design an annual session for novitiates in Pakistan to be conducted in both English and Urdu! Electronic sources make this even easier for two reasons:

- Local online publications are easily read internationally.
- Submission and publication are ridiculously easy.

The stature and credibility of local hardcopy and electronic publications are increased tremendously through "international expertise." That's you.

"Speak" locally

Teleconferences are very valuable because they can become MP3 downloads, CDs, streaming audio on websites, and so forth. These take two very worthwhile forms:

- You are interviewed by someone with a regular audience and broadcast schedule. This builds your role as the "expert," and is easier than falling off a chair (which Alan has done during his teleconferences—twice).
- You initiate the teleconference using your lists and faithful followers, which people may join "live," listen to by phone on recording, listen to by subsequent download, obtain transcriptions—you get the idea. The leverage is huge.

Without leaving your office, your voice can reach people all over the globe.

"Appear" locally

Alan tapes a video at his home to be broadcast monthly. He does five at a time, which cost—in total—about US$500, including cameraman and assistant, lights, sound, editing, and final version for digital viewing. The series, *The Writing on the Wall*, is on his website, blog, and YouTube. Thus, there are three outlets for people to watch him talk on management, strategy, leadership, current events, social change, and so forth. Each runs about eight minutes. (The YouTube limit for uploads is ten minutes!) You can find them here if you'd like to see samples, which are also archived on his website: <http://summitconsulting.com/>.

One of Omar's global clients has him run what it calls "achievement cultivators:" One-day focus sessions on a particular area of leadership or management expertise that is most needed or desired by it at that time. It builds up enthusiasm for these internally through video vignettes of Omar delivering on these topics on its website, and by having a one-page article by him appear quarterly in its global newsletter. When he then travels to its locations, he's welcomed as someone the audiences recognize and feel they have already interacted with.

Sell locally

Both hardcopy products and electronic downloads sell well internationally. If you are truly interested in global consulting, you should launch products in print and audio (video does not sell as well) to attract international attention and allow you to be purchased "locally." The key here includes to resist examples that are only appropriate for you locally; to avoid obvious comments about time and current events; and deliberately to include a variety of issues appealing to internationalists. (If you're an American talking about 401k plans or health care, you're not going to be as appealing as when you discuss international trade and intellectual property rights.)

Your intellectual property and brand can take many forms. Projecting them to others is the key to being considered a "local" resource, even though you may be 12,000 miles away. You also begin to create a desirability about demanding your physical presence, which can rely on a critical mass of prospects and even existing long-range clients. It's one thing to fly from Rome to Cape Town for an hour's speech, but quite another to spend a week there, with three speeches, a consulting day, two people to coach, a book-signing event, and the opportunity to market personally for future business as well. (As this is written, Alan has worked in Sydney nine months ahead, representing nearly US$80,000 in business with expenses paid, before the major publicity being launched!)

Omar recently had a week in which he did US$65,000 of business, with a day and a half in London, a day in Amsterdam, a day in Copenhagen, and finished up with a speech in Zurich. Different locations, but roughly an hour's flight in between each, and not bad for a focused week!

The local alliance

There is a difference between an alliance and a subcontractor. It's a vital difference, especially since you will be a "remote" partner.

A subcontractor delivers, executes, implements. That means that you assign the implementation for business you've already sold to a local person. His or her role might include:

- teaching a class
- speaking or presenting
- coaching or counseling
- delivering a report or performing research
- running focus groups
- conducting 360° feedback sessions
- conducting interviews
- administering surveys
- observing an operation or performance
- facilitating a meeting
- and so forth...

You get the idea. These are your local hands and feet on the ground. You typically pay a daily rate. It's vital to understand that these are quite often people who cannot market themselves. They have significant talent, but not selling ability. They are quite plentiful, truth be told.

Since it's a buyer's market, you should never overpay these people, because they will erode your profit margins. Don't listen to the erroneous refrain that your programs depend on the quality that only the person speaking to you can possibly bring to bear. It's untrue. Good help is all around. (To give you a point of comparison: In the U.S., it's not unusual for large seminar companies to pay their subcontract instructors as little as US$300 per day. That is not a misprint: *US$300 per day!*)

An alliance partner is different. An alliance partner is a local person or firm that provides help in the acquisition of business or the methodology or technology employed. He, she, or it may or may not also take part in delivery and execution. This is different than a subcontractor.

Alliance partners provide a marketing competitive edge. In some parts of the world, you must have a local alliance partner, often one that "owns" 51 percent or more of the venture (China comes to mind). In most parts of the world, however, the relationship is whatever the two of you determine it will be.

Alliances are like marriages. They create great romance at the outset, but can be dogged fights to the finish if there is need for a breakup. Therefore, we recommend the following crucible for analyzing alliance partners:

- Meet personally with the principals. Do you like and trust them? Meet under varied conditions.
- Perform due diligence. Talk to their employees, clients, bankers, and suppliers. If possible, do a background check, including criminal activity and suits pending.
- Are they bringing money to the table? Do they already have clients who would benefit from your technology and approaches?
- Do they provide unique assets, such as multiple language and translation ability, government contacts, a training center, people in multiple countries, and so on?
- Are your approaches compatible and synergistic with theirs? Do they represent others who might conflict with you? How much attention and focus will you receive?
- Can you reach financial arrangements that make sense, for example, your control of receipts, using your currency drawn on banks in your country, no obligation for local expenses, and so forth?

Global learning

If you confuse a subcontract employee with an alliance partner, you will be paying the doorman as though he owned the building.

There are three parts or dynamics to any customer business: acquisition, methodology, and delivery. Although there are three, they are not equal in representations. Our division looks like this:

- Acquisition: 50 percent of the revenue.
- Methodology or technology: 30 percent of the revenue.
- Delivery or execution: 20 percent of the revenue.

So in a US$100,000 sale, where you close the business, we use my technology, and you deliver, you would receive US$70,000 and I would receive US$30,000, and I would never have to show up. If we both closed the sale, used my technology, and you delivered, you would receive US$45,000 and I would receive US$65,000, and I would probably have been there for the sales process. (Note that if it's my sale and my technology, then this isn't an alliance but a subcontracting relationship, and I should *not* be providing you with 20 percent of the proceeds, but only a daily rate. That is a key distinction to bear in mind.)

Realize that your subcontractors don't have to be "on the ground"—we have scaled up for a US$250,000 coaching project by importing associates from Dubai, Sri Lanka, and London, and used Australians for a variety of Pacific Rim projects. If the talent profile and your positioning are right, and the value to the client is significant, getting the right people isn't a barrier.

You can create a presence first by building client relationships that transcend distance, and by being convenient to contact and fast to get a response from. Looking for associates who are on the ground can create a cost-effective delivery mechanism with, hopefully, local insight—as long as it's your brand and intellectual capital. However, creating a pool of delivery associates (subcontractors) also lets you potentially bid for jobs anywhere—if you can demonstrate you're fielding a "dream team" (implementation-wise) for a particular undertaking.

You are best off piloting an alliance first, on a single project and single client. Beware of people who want to "partner," but bring nothing to the table except their physical presence. They simply want to "partner" money out of your pocket and into theirs. The genuine alliance partner candidates will view the relationship in this manner:

- You can bring multinational, prior business to influence local sites of those multinationals.
- Your role as "knowledge exporter" increases their profile and credibility.
- You provide a technology or methodology that allows them to enrich their existing clients.
- They will use your physical presence to launch special marketing events, speeches, appointments, media publicity, and so forth.
- There is a win (you), win (them), win (clients) mentality manifest.

Great alliance partners are hard to find, but easy to nurture once found. Alan has US$85,000 in business already set up and being paid for in Australia in nine months solely through alliance partners.

In January, Omar was able to use alliance partners in a sub-contracting capacity to deliver three key engagements for him. Omar spent 30 minutes providing guidance, and these alliance partners knew the approach and material he used well enough for that to suffice. The billing was US$40,000 for the three sessions. Omar paid US$9,000 to his colleagues (their full day rates), and racked up US$31,000 in a little more than two weeks for having a brand that attracted business without having to show up or do anything further.

Physical presence

We don't want to create the impression that global consulting is about never actually crossing a border. There are good reasons to schlep through airport security, transit a few time zones, and pack your laptop. Among them:

- You gain the pleasure, growth, and learning of the diverse global landscape. This is particularly valuable if you have family, friends, or significant others who wish to share this with you. (We'll discuss this aspect in greater depth in Chapter 12, "Life Balance.")
- Credibility is tremendously boosted by having the first-hand experience and understanding of local culture.

- Some executives would consider it inappropriate and disrespectful to conduct business without a personal meeting at the outset.
- You want to avoid cognitive dissonance, and want what you are told also to be what you see and hear.
- You can combine sales, marketing, implementation, and relationship building on single trips.

Here is an immutable law of the global consulting universe: If you are based in New York and tell someone in Philadelphia that you are going to be in town, he or she may or may not make the time on his or her calendar to see you. If you tell that to someone in San Francisco, he or she will probably change his or her schedule to provide time for you. If you tell that to someone in Hong Kong, he or she will probably offer to host a dinner and set up various meetings.

Global learning

There is a direct proportion between the distance you travel and the receptivity of the person you wish to visit!

We had a colleague in the profession who lived in Connecticut, and would catch the Concorde from New York in the morning, conduct business in London, and catch the evening flight back. He thought he was being efficient.

We thought he was out of his mind.

It's not the wear-and-tear aspect (although the speed of the Concorde days are gone), but the opportunities lost. If you are going over a border, plan to use the time intelligently. In many cultures, socialization is as important as business dealings. When Alan consulted at length in Mexico, he couldn't avoid 6:30 a.m. games of tennis on an office rooftop, nor 9 p.m. dinners with colleagues and staff, nor midnight excursions for tripe ladled out of earthen pots. Japanese clients, with their insistence on heavy alcoholic consumption, are far worse.

Omar remembers being served camel meat by an Arab sheikh who had sponsored a major speech by Omar at a global conference, in traditional style—that is, he broke off the meat with his right hand, and quite ceremoniously deposited it on Omar's plate. Next came aromatic rice, served the same way, and round the platter went. Asking for a salad would not have been a prudent option! That said, the meat and rice were truly luscious.

Here is our formula for the most productive and satisfying local presence when you travel to other countries.

- Combine visits. It's silly to travel from London and make separate trips to Rome and Madrid. Combine them on one trip.

- Travel light. That sounds counterintuitive, but you can ship luggage ahead, buy disposable products locally, or keep things permanently in storage in locations you repeatedly visit. Lindsay Fox, the CEO of Linfox Trucking in Australia, was famous for keeping a duplicate set of clothing in a Sydney hotel, matching his Melbourne wardrobe. Charles Wrigley, of the chewing gum empire, kept identical clothing in every one of his residences. You don't have to be that zealous, but you get the idea.

- Plan your stay to maximize fitness and effectiveness:
  - Allow a day to acclimatize.
  - Use limos, not cabs, for safe, clean, and on-time service.
  - Choose a hotel with a health club, and use it daily.
  - Allow plenty of time between visits and appointments.
  - Build in "down time" every day.
  - Eat local food with discretion until you adjust as necessary.
  - Make excuses to hosts and others, but limit the length of your daily activities.
  - Don't make tight flight connections in transit or in departing after your final meetings.
  - Travel first class if at all possible, business class at worst. The extra cost is more than justified by the boost to your comfort and wellbeing.

    (Also, remember that all first-class perks aren't equal, particularly outside North America. For example, if flying into London, while British Airways and Emirates have a comparable first-class product in the air on various routes, Emirates provides a complimentary chauffeur-driven service within a three-hour drive of Heathrow or Gatwick. On a round-trip basis, compared with a car service, that can be a saving of more than US$400. On the other hand, if your hotel room won't be ready for several hours because you're landing early, British Airways has an arrivals lounge, where you can shower, get your clothes pressed, have a hot breakfast, get all major papers, use the Internet, get a complimentary massage, and even find repose in a meditation room! This is far better than languishing in a hotel lobby feeling like something the proverbial cat dragged in. Knowing these things as you travel helps. This isn't about sybaritic luxury, although treating yourself well doesn't need justification. It's about effectiveness, getting prudent value out of your first-class investment, and being aware of the facilities you can avail yourself of to make your traveling life easier and better.)

- Make sure you learn something about the country and participate in nonbusiness events while there.
- A good hotel will have a concierge who will print boarding passes and arrange for all local requirements. (Be sure to tip appropriately at the conclusion of your stay. In the U.K., this person is known as the "hall porter.")

• Take your laptop and a good international cell phone. (We've found that the iPhone is superb.) You can stay in touch these days with minimal expense and effort. Alan calls clients from the beach, and Omar from the ski slopes. We advise against taking only a PDA or "light" laptop. You may need to create a proposal, open large attachments, create graphics, and so on.

Here's our typical stay in, for example, Buenos Aires:

Day one:
Arrival: acclimatization, nap, workout, recreation
  7:00 Dinner with local business colleagues

Day two:
  7:00 Wake-up call. Watching CNN while getting ready
  8:00 Breakfast with local alliance partner or subcontractors
  9:30 Implementation at client, lunch with buyer
  6:00 Catching up on email and phone calls from home
  7:00 Workout or massage
  8:30 Dinner with friends or client

Day three:
  7:00 Wake-up call. Watching Bloomberg Business News Network
  8:00 Breakfast with potential alliance partner or subcontractor
10:00 Speech at local trade association

12:00 Down time: calls, recreation, email
 1:30 Lunch with trade association board members
 3:00 Visiting prospect set up by local people
 4:30 Visiting second prospect set up through Internet
 6:00 Workout or massage
 8:30 Dinner with friends or client

Day four:
 7:00 Wake-up call. Watching MSNBC while getting ready
 8:00 Breakfast alone
 9:30 Wrapping up emails and phone calls locally and from home
11:00 Final meeting with plans for future with partners, sub-
         contractors
 1:00 Limo to airport
 2:30 Lunch in airport club
 4:00 Departing flight

You get the idea. You can create a productive but nonstressful trip involving personal goals, health, prospects, clients, partners, and so on. That makes local presence also a local pleasure.

The local, formal office

The ultimate creation of presence is a permanent representation. In other words, you have assets and infrastructure, local phone, mail, and so on.

That seems like a huge commitment, and it is. Alan has never done it, Omar has, and others we know have been both successful and unsuccessful in so doing.

Even though Omar has used this option, it has been reluctantly, and only when there were a preponderance of reasons (see in the following) that made a strong case for doing so.

Here are the questions to ask to determine whether a "fixed" asset makes sense:

- Does the potential business in the immediate and wider geographical area justify (or necessitate) a formal office and operation?
- Does the local law demand this presence once a certain financial threshold is achieved?

- Do you require or prefer local facilities that cannot be provided by an alliance partner or third party (for example, shared business facilities)?
- Does your business require unique equipment or on-site configurations (for example, specialized training or video conferencing).
- Is it less expensive to own or rent than to use others' property?
- Will this create an equity investment for the future if you sell or sublet?
- Will it help repatriate funds to your home country?
- Will it create a better image and more appeal in a competitive marketplace?
- Will it improve and promote your brand?
- Does it provide a tax advantage?
- Are you personally on site enough to use it to advantage?
- Are you reasonably certain it will be safe and managed by trustworthy people?
- Can it represent you in the general area, for example Southeast Asia, as opposed to solely one location, for example Bangkok?
- Can you obtain cost-effective insurance and security?
- Do you have cost-effective financing options for purchase or rent and upkeep?

If you can respond positively to at least 12 of these questions, then you probably have good reason to consider the formal, local office. In many places, such as Japan, Korea, Romania, and other countries, you must have a local partner, often a majority partner, if you intend to conduct a high level of local business. When that's the case, the partner's offices and facilities will almost always make more sense. Other locations like Hong Kong, Singapore and Dubai require *either* a local partner *or* a physical address, or both. In that case, you have to weigh the relative advantages, aggravations, and upsides carefully in deciding which to plump for.

As nice as it is to have a place you can call "home away from home," we've found that it's often unnecessary to have an office *in your native country*. Omar has used a virtual office for years, and Alan has made it a point of working out of his home since he founded his company. Therefore, the utility of an office overseas is far from a no brainer. We've worked with and for true international consulting firms with offices abroad (at one time, Alan managed Asia and Latin America for a Princeton-based consulting firm). It's not as impressive as it sounds:

- The offices were often bare-bones and poorly supported, just an excuse to cite a local office and provide a local address. Virtually no work was done there.
- The work that often was done locally, for example printing or distribution, could easily be done from a central point in a digital age of "print on demand" and email circulation.
- Local taxes and even local bribes became necessary just by dint of physical presence, not in proportion to any business being conducted.
- It is sometimes nigh on impossible to fire anyone hired locally because of arcane employment laws. We once endured a two-year acrimonious wait to fire a local director in Germany, and then only with an onerous legal settlement; it required a year to relieve a Japanese manager; and six months to remove an administrative assistant in Brazil (who then took all the office records with her).
- It's not uncommon for local people, disgruntled or "entrepreneurial," to appropriate local materials, mailing lists, goodwill, and even physical assets, and go into competition with you. The recourse to the law across boundaries is slow, torturous, expensive, and seldom effective.

Consider that in most cases consulting involved the transfer of advice and the provision of a "sounding board." That never takes place in the consultant's office. (As Alan's wife, Maria, observed when he began his own business, and wanted to look for an office: "Why do you need an office? No one is going to come to you." Although they do come to him now, they come electronically, and when they come physically, they come to his home.)

In other words, you will be visiting client sites. You should be comfortable in an excellent hotel. If a client needs to see you off site, the hotel can easily arrange a conference room or you can take a two-room suite for that purpose. Local alliance partners can supply office space for infrequent meetings. There are also universal clubs that you can join and access these facilities all over the word. The Regus Clubs are just one example.

In summary, here's how best to establish local "presence" without a physical office for the vast majority of you who will never need one or can't answer positively to a dozen of the questions we posed:

Global learning

A physical office is the most expensive, time consuming, and difficult global presence, and is less required than ever in a digital age.

- Use local alliance partners or subcontractors.
- Provide articles, columns, and interviews for local publications.
- Make planned visits with events scheduled to highlight your presence.
- Send out local press releases.
- Sponsor local events.
- Provide teleconferences, webinars, or podcasts for the area.
- Establish a powerful brand.
- Have physical products, preferably in the local language and English.
- Be willing to accommodate phone calls at odd hours to create access.
- Return email inquiries and correspondence rapidly (within one business day).
- Use Fedex or another reliable courier service. Don't rely on the mail service.
- For consistency, use the same hotel or temporary office every time you come.

The less infrastructure the better, and you're conducting a global consulting business in a world that has come to embrace virtual presence fully.

World tour

- Working with the local people can involve differing degrees of involvement.

- You can project your image and your brand from long distances.

- The export of knowledge and expertise is your fundamental value.

- Elevate and intensify your local presence as business justifies it or regulations require.

- The fundamental dynamic is that you will go to the client, be it physically or virtually, so do that as effectively and cost effectively as possible.

Part II

The Itinerary

Chapter 4

Requisites for Success: Material

Creating your own time machine

So what do you need to "span the globe," and enjoy the thrill of victory without the agony of defeat?[1] If you want to avoid the fate of that iconographic ski jumper in the opening sequence of *Wide World of Sports*, we have some suggestions for your equipment, support, and lifestyle.

Staying on top of your game

When you must physically travel, you can do so in a myriad of alternate ways while keeping your wits about you. We're going to tread a thin hedonistic line here, and you'll find what's on the far side of that line in the appendices, which cover our best recommendations on food, drink, recreation, arts, and so on. But for now, consider us on the side of the line dealing with self-preservation and renewal.

Here are 17 ways to stay in the best possible mental shape. Don't forget that you will often be dealing with gracious hosts who are also sharp business minds or executives who operate in a culture where you are naturally expected to drive the best deal possible.

In other words, charm ain't never enough. (That was Alan. Omar probably would have said, charm is like oxygen to a fire, necessary but not sufficient. Either way, you know what we mean.)

17 ways to stay mentally and physically fit

1. Travel first class or at least business class

Some airlines have a business class as their best class of service, and it's wonderful. Virgin Airlines comes to mind, with its seats that do a ballet and transform themselves into comfortable beds, complete with thick pillows and duvets. There are also a manicurist and massage therapist available.

Some airlines have a magnificent first class, such as Singapore Air and Emirates, but also have outstanding business-class service. Other airlines are mediocre or erratic in both areas. Delta and United come to mind.

Don't choose flights merely by ease of schedule. Look into securing the very best service your finances allow. Alan, while working for a penurious consulting firm as a bottom-runger, once had to take a ten-hour flight to Rio in the middle of five seats in coach, in the smoking section, of an MD-10 jumbo. On another occasion, an ancient Japan Air 707 took off with people standing in the aisles, and landed in Manila so hard that all the oxygen masks fell out.

Global learning

If you don't take care of yourself, you can't take care of others or of business, of family or of clients. That's why they tell you on the plane, "Always put your own oxygen mask on first before trying to help others."

Virgin Airlines will send a limo to your door (if you're within 50 miles of the airport), and deliver you to your hotel at the other end, reversing the process on the way back. They also expedite your passage through customs and immigration, and have what's generally voted to be the finest air club in the world in Heathrow near London.

Alan traveled first class from the moment he went out on his own, considering it a normal business expense, no less than telephone or office supplies. Years ago, an employee of a strategic ally of Omar's was shocked to find that Omar routinely traveled first class, on the same rationale as Alan. But it so upset this person's financial miserliness that he burst out to Omar's strategic ally, "How can you *trust* someone who flies first class?" The assumption came from the fact presumably, to paraphrase George Bernard Shaw, that some people think they are being moral when they are uncomfortable. Well, we disagree with both the dubious morality, as well as with courting the "effectiveness backlash" you'll experience if you pride yourself on how well you can traumatize yourself during travel. You must travel comfortably and be able to rest. (The Concorde was fascinating and fast, but as uncomfortable as you can imagine in narrow seats for more than three hours, top-flight scotch notwithstanding.)

2. Hire limos

Taxis are notoriously dirty, in poor repair, and driven by nonprofessionals in most cities (London being a clear exception). Moreover, you can't always depend on finding one, inclement weather presents a problem, and in some countries there are security issues.

Ask your host, alliance partner, or hotel concierge to recommend a good limo company, and use them from dawn to dusk. In places such as Rio or Quito, it will have identification, which will be checked by hotel security. In Bangkok, we rented a new Volvo with professional driver for US$24 for the day, and the limo-service owners checked back with us when we returned to the hotel early to ensure that we weren't unhappy. (We were just ahead of schedule.)

It's particularly important to have limo transportation from and to overseas airports. Firms, such as Carey International, provide corporate accounts and worldwide service, and are very reliable.

(Note: You don't travel this way in "high risk" countries, such as Colombia.)

3. Use top-rated hotels

You don't have to stay in The Four Seasons in Santiago, but you can stay in the Sheraton, which is a wonderful place. (You'll find that many brands are of different quality in different places, so that Sheraton is a mid-range brand in the U.S., but a much better brand overseas.)

Specifically, use hotels that feature:

- full-service concierge support
- excellent security
- health and fitness clubs
- several different restaurants

- 24-hour door service
- wireless Internet
- on-site currency exchange
- basic stores (newspapers, toiletries, refreshments)
- a staffed business center

Better hotels that get to know you (and if you return to the same cities, it behooves you to forge such relationships) will receive mail for you, obtain difficult restaurant and theater reservations, provide public spaces for meetings, and even keep a list in their database of your preferred magazines, complimentary beverages, pillow types, and more. Feeling as though you're returning to a surrogate "home" makes the emotional landing that much better, and you know that the practicalities of business and life will be well handled and supported.

4. Schedule acclimatization days

You'll often arrive in the morning overseas, but even if you arrive in the evening, take the next day off. You need your internal clock to reset, and you also must take into consideration the likelihood of:

- airplane delays
- immigration and customs delays
- lost luggage
- local labor strikes
- hotel reservation mix-ups
- weather problems
- personal illness

An acclimatization day provides the ability to deal with these issues or, if none occurs, visit a museum, check out the city, prepare for your meetings, buy gifts,[2] or treat yourself to a spa or salon.

On the other end, don't schedule a return flight too close to a business meeting or other obligation. Our advice is to get a good night's sleep, and depart in mid-morning, schedules permitting. (You haven't lived until you've been picked up at 4 a.m. in Quito to be whisked in the dark of night to a poorly staffed airport by a driver who apparently speaks no known language.)

You don't have to be a pack animal

5. Travel light

When we go somewhere for a few days, we try to take just carry-on bags. However, if you're traveling for a longer period, and need more "stuff," then consider this:

- FedEx your luggage ahead of time. It costs more, but it speeds your trip and creates far less hassle for you. (Many airlines are now restricting weights or charging penalties, so FedEx is looking better and better. There are some companies that specialize in luggage delivery by courier, as well.) We have been fans of sending bags ahead of time for years. This can also help avoid the stress of tight flight connections, and save up to an hour in baggage claim when you hopefully have other things to get on with.

    If you travel frequently to the same city, you can "domesticate" specific hotels, as we've said, to help with this. Sometimes, it is wise to upgrade the quality of hotel based pragmatically on what you may want from it beyond a room for the night. Omar has to frequently travel for ongoing consulting work to Asia Pacific and to the U.K. and E.U. His preferred hotels in Singapore (Raffles) and in London (the Four Seasons) each keep a permanent bag for him. That way, if he has to head directly from Singapore to Geneva, his bag can be couriered by the London hotel to Geneva, with clothes appropriate to Europe in hand, awaiting his arrival.
- Your hotel can arrange for various sundries and toiletries, from razors to mouthwash, and bathing suits to shoe repair. There is no need to pack small items (especially liquids, which cause security problems) that you can find or buy on site.

6. Keep your key personal needs with you

Obviously, never pack medication in checked luggage, even that which you may only need sporadically, because flights are sometimes delayed by hours and luggage, is often lost. ("Your luggage is not lost," a Thai employee of Qantas Airways told Alan, "we simply don't know where it is at the moment.") You may just need those antacid tablets when you least suspect it.

However, many people don't realize that they should take copies of their eyeglass or contact-lens prescriptions; medical prescriptions; a photocopy of the opening pages of their passports; and various emergency call numbers, all packed in a safe place in their briefcase (and, for the truly paranoid, duplicated and also stowed in one's carry-on luggage). Other rarely needed but very useful items:

Global learning

Ironically, the most troublesome events are the relatively minor ones. Your hotel staff can provide a physician, the airline can arrange an alternate flight, but you'd better be prepared to deal with broken eyeglasses, which could undermine the rest of your trip.

- a "Fixodent" type of paste to temporarily replace a bridge or veneer that has come loose. (Alan lost a crown once just as he was being introduced to speak in Singapore.)
- extra batteries for hearing aids, minirecorders, and other items that require nonstandard batteries
- emery boards to take care of a cracked nail or ugly hangnails
- a tiny eyeglass repair kit, which includes a small screwdriver, magnifying glass, and screws.

7. Be a smart, high-tech traveler

It's increasingly easy to obtain electricity converters and adapters wherever you go. However, here are some ideas to make your travels as productive and efficient as possible:

- For any extended trip, take your laptop so that you can write proposals, open lengthy attachments, create invoices, check email easily, and so forth. Pack a converter that will power the computer on the airplane, because most long-distance planes now have onboard power outlets.
- Make sure your cell phone is easily and readily adaptable for international use without having to make separate arrangements in each country you visit. (The absolute best and easiest phone we've seen is the iPhone, which dials normally wherever you take it.[3])
- Japan, as we've found out ruefully, operates on a distinct cellular network, and to have cell-phone access even with global roaming, you need a triband phone. This may not be

relevant to many, but the point is that it's important to be literate in the basics of where you are going: phone connections, voltages, computer access, and more.

- Ensure that you have all of your passwords for Internet access with you, and all bookmarks that are on your home or desktop system as well.
- The use of a wireless connector, such as the Verizon USB device that plugs into a laptop, will provide access to the Internet and email wherever cell phones can be used. This will enable you to access email and the web during a long day of calls, if you're taking your laptop with you and there is no other easy connection. Having a global roaming connection service is also important in many Wi-Fi spots that aren't free in their access. Check your provider, and select one that has top-notch reciprocal arrangements, so you can use time in train stations, airport lounges, coffee shops, and more to good advantage.

8. Provide local materials

During an assignment for State Street Bank some years ago, Alan was to help determine why international approaches were or were not being consistently applied in local offices. The last place he expected to find problems was "right across the pond" in London, his first stop.

However, there was great discontent in the London office. The local management dropped the bank's very prestigious brochure on the desk.

"Have you seen this?" he was asked.

"Of course," he said, "it's a nice piece, and very consistent."

"Right. Now read the rear cover."

It took three readings before Alan realized that the brochure suggested to the affluent British investor who might be expected to read this that he or she, if interested in next steps, contact the bank: *at the Boston address and phone number!* The brochure had never been vetted for international use, just printed in the tens of thousands!

Wherever possible, change your collateral, promotional, and implementation materials so that local examples, frames of reference, and actions are accommodated. If practical, have materials translated by a reputable source or alliance partner.

(Alan's books are in eight languages, with more coming, including Russian, Chinese, Arabic, and Korean.)

9. Choose your time of day and location

Don't just accept meeting times and dates. We've already suggested that a day of acclimatization is needed. But times of day can be critical to your wellbeing. Negotiating rush hour traffic in, say, Mexico City, or Cairo, or Bangkok, or Rio, or New Delhi, or Hong Kong, can make Los Angeles and New York roads seem abandoned and empty.

Similarly, choose sites that make sense. There may be a beautiful retreat house 40 miles outside of Haifa, but if it requires three hours to get there and three hours to get back, you've sacrificed a day and a lot of energy for what should have been a 90-minute meeting. Try to choose business environments as well. Going out with your Japanese hosts for sushi, beer, and sake in the evening is definitely *not* going to be conducive to business negotiations (at least negotiations that will be remembered the next morning). Moreover, the tobacco smoke will in all probability be horrible.

10. Join every club that you reasonably can

We've talked elsewhere in this book about business clubs that can accommodate your meetings or relaxation around the world. It's also a necessity to join as many airline clubs as possible.[4] Some airlines will accept a third-party card, such as American Express Platinum. These clubs provide fine food, massages, showers, international communications, and staff who can change flights or accommodations.

We've both been in situations in which one club wasn't appropriate or helpful, but another was. First-class travelers are treated like royalty on most international airlines. These clubs are fantastic investments.

When things go "bump" in the night

11. Prepare your contingency plans

We've been "stuck" more times than we have room to report here. Suffice it to say that fog can delay flights by days in

London; spontaneous air traffic controller strikes can ground planes for days in Sydney; and local inefficiencies can create bureaucratic problems, which can prevent you from getting to, or through, the airport in time for your flight.

Never travel without backup plans. What is the next flight you can use? What is an alternate hotel to stay at? Do you have the client's cell-phone number? Do you have your limo driver's cell-phone number (and his company number, and the hotel number)? Can you get copies of key documents sent by courier? What access do you have to your travel agent?

Build a great relationship with a travel agent who can and will act decisively on your behalf. Omar was traveling back to Copenhagen airport from Elsinore (the location of Hamlet's castle) after a two-day senior leadership retreat for Svitzer (a subsidiary of the shipping giant Maersk). Looking at his ticket, he noticed to his chagrin that the date on it was the next day. He realized that the session had shifted by a day, and he had neglected to let his travel agent know.

Global learning

Preventive action is always the most critical, so plan carefully, but hope for the best and plan for the worst. The safest buildings still have fire extinguishers on the walls.

Omar called his travel agent from the car. The travel agent said he would have to reissue a new ticket, and get the old one refunded later—something he could handle at his end without bothering Omar's plans. Fortunately, a first-class seat was still available, and 20 minutes later, by the time Omar pulled up to Copenhagen airport, the e-ticket was in the system, and he was able to check in and head off without delay or inconvenience.

If you're sitting in the airport, trapped in your hotel, or held prisoner by traffic with no control over your fate, you only have yourself to blame. God created technology so that you could have backup plans.

12. Use travel agents, not your keyboard

One of the great myths of the electronic age is that all travel planning can be done online. Our experience is that the amount of money saved is not always as great as we're led to believe, but also that a "live" intermediary can often be priceless.

When you travel domestically, a local travel agent is often sufficient. Occasionally, even internationally they suffice (as in the example given) when the time zone gods are smiling on you. But because of time differences, that relationship doesn't work when it's 11:00 p.m. back home but you need help in Jakarta in the early morning. The remedy we've found is "round the clock" help, such as that you can acquire from American Express Platinum. This is an amenity that you can intensify by finding the names of a few people (the same one won't always be on duty) and the best local numbers to call to access help. You'll have a record of your preferences as well.

Once, during a terrible electrical storm in St. Louis, Alan found himself stranded in the airport near midnight, arriving several hours late and missing his connection to Branson, where he was to speak late the next morning. Every local hotel was rumored to be full, with crowds in the lobbies. Alan called American Express on his cell, and the agent took ten minutes to obtain a suite at a suburban Ritz–Carlton for US$135, and arranged for a new connection in the morning in time for his speech. He took a cab to the hotel, walked around a large group trying to get rooms, showed his card to an assistant manager, and bypassed the rush. He managed six hours of sleep, and the hotel car returned him to the airport the next day.

There are other options to Amex (and Platinum status is not difficult to achieve), but you get the idea. Alan opening his laptop and finding some Internet travel help would have been problematic, uncomfortable, and nowhere near as rapid.

Another time, Omar and his wife were making that trip to Ireland we wrote about earlier. Of all things, Dubai airport was fogged in. Omar, in addition to Amex Platinum, uses a global concierge service that also operates 24 hours (<www.quintessentially.com>) for such situations. Sitting on the tarmac, Omar called it, and was routed to its London office, also operative 24 hours a day. It told him there was another flight he and Leslie could take the next morning (about an hour after the one they were now clearly going to miss). Quintessentially not only booked them onto that next flight as their plane was taking off from Dubai, but also called and informed their car service in Ireland, and even updated their hotel on their new expected arrival time. Since Omar and Leslie only had carry-on (see our advice on this earlier in the chapter), they made their connection in the 45 minutes they had—something that would otherwise have been virtually impossible at Heathrow with twice the time.

13. Virtual assistants can be real

Virtual assistants come in two types: The very helpful, and those who lose business for you. The astounding aspect is that you determine which kind you have!

Find someone, through references of colleagues, who isn't doing this to pick up some money between sending the kids to school and working at a beauty salon. Find someone for whom this is a *profession*. Would you choose a part-time mechanic for your car, or a part-time teacher for your child, or a part-time physician for your health, all of whom were holding down radically different jobs "on the side"?

We didn't think so.

It's unreasonable to expect your virtual assistant to be personally available 24 hours a day during your travels, but it is reasonable to expect the following, at a minimum:

- Take calls and messages and promptly respond in your absence.
- Review and respond to appropriate email, leave the remainder for you to answer from the road.[5]
- Pay periodic and expectable bills online, for business purposes (for example, magazine subscriptions or club memberships, maximum authorized amounts US$350).
- Take care of both planned and emergency travel requirements. This is especially useful as you encounter surprises during your business meetings.
- Create form letters, invoices, acknowledgments, reminders, and so on to be sent. For example, an electronic reminder of meetings in the next 24 or 48 hours going to your clients and prospects and alliance partners helps to prevent problems. ("I didn't realize you would be here in the morning; thanks for the reminder.")

You can expect to pay anywhere from US$250 to more than US$1,000 for a good virtual assistant. If you don't have an office or staff, this can be a vital global consulting investment. (Note: If you are using a spouse or significant other for this, be aware that he or she has to appreciate the supportive nature of the role, and not treat it as "when I have the time to get around to it." We've seen relationships suffer under that strain.)

14. Virtual offices can be real

Omar is famous for setting up "instant offices," often at the bottom of a ski slope or overlooking a golf course. If you can *intelligently* set up some combination of cell phone, laptop, PDA, and other aids (digital camera for a blog entry, for example), you can be "in business" for an hour while sipping hot chocolate or savoring cognac.

This may sound as though you were "traveling heavy," but you're really not, especially in terms of tradeoff for productivity. Alan is usually taking hobby photos anyway, and also uses them for his website, blog, and forum. Omar tracks everything on his PDA from stocks to flight delays. Since both of us write, a laptop is *de rigueur* for trips, but it also serves to create proposals, invoices, and the normal correspondence necessary to put money in the bank instantly. (Providing a prospect with a proposal immediately after a meeting and then reviewing it the next day certainly beat a week's delay when you are halfway around the world.)

All of the accoutrements can fit into your briefcase if you do it right. There is another huge advantage: When you have unexpected down time (flight canceled, business meeting canceled, and so on), you are instantly productive, right on the spot.

There's feeling good and looking good

15. Manage the lag

Jetlag is real. For us, it's worse going west to east, but it strikes people in various ways. It's always a huge issue when you're heading off for business, but don't underestimate its effects when you're returning home.

If your family hasn't seen you for a week or more, do you really want to sleep for 20 hours immediately upon returning home (or fall asleep during the kids' soccer game or sound like a babbling idiot at the fundraiser reception)?

There are quite a few good books and pamphlets on the subject, so we've simply listed our favorite anti-jetlag preventives and remedies over a combined seven million air miles of travel:

- Keep hydrated. Drink a lot of water. Yes, it will prompt trips to the restroom. It's a small price to pay, and another reason to travel first class.
- Don't overdo the alcohol. A glass of wine isn't likely to hurt you, but too much booze on the flight will undermine your rest, and too much booze with clients (who are more accustomed to the practice locally) will undermine your business.
- Use appropriate sleep aids. Most first-class or business-class airline kits will include earplugs and eye shades, and you'll have a comfortable pillow and "bed." You can also buy inflatable neck supports and sound soothers to play through your earplugs. (Some airlines provide pajamas and very private beds; Emirates currently provides separate cabins in first class and the new Airbus A-380 that Singapore Airlines has been the first to roll out even has "suites for two.")
- Exercise. Make sure you use a hotel with this amenity. Don't go running through the streets, even in the safest of places. But do get your blood pumping.
- Get a massage. Excellent massages are easy to obtain around the world, and they can be of tremendous help to work through sore muscles, remove toxins, and create peace.

We've spoken elsewhere of taking time to acclimatize. For example, Alan will arrive in London at about 9 a.m., have the hotel provide early check-in for 10:30 a.m. (after immigration), take a nap, get a massage, have dinner with friends, and then get a "normal" night's sleep.

16. Manage the image

Get your shoes shone, have your business clothing pressed, get a facial, book a manicure, and take care of your hair. That's right, pamper yourself even more than you do at home.

We've seen international travelers who look as though they had to stand during the flight and walked from the airport into town. They aren't just bedraggled by travel; they are poorly groomed through bad taste. We don't care where you are, you shouldn't be in an airline club, hotel lounge, or other public place in shorts, flip-flops, and tee-shirt, male or female, whatever age, if you're a businessperson.

This is for your own emotional wellbeing, not just the image you portray to others. We all know the great feeling we get from a new suit or great haircut.

There are excellent, wrinkle-resistant choices in clothing today, often from top designers. Alan's choice is almost always black Armani, which is always in style, always appropriate, and great for photos. He wears the suit with a black open-collar shirt, a black turtleneck sweater, or a white shirt and red tie, depending on the circumstances. If he has to, he can travel on the plane that way, although he prefers not to (usually designer jeans and a collared shirt, so that you are comfortable but still look well put together).

Omar's personal preference for a suit that looks good and travels well is from his tailor, Kilgour French in London's famed Savile Row, matched with colorful shirts from Turnbull & Asser, which are available now in New York as readily as in London. For the plane, Omar will wear a nice mock turtleneck, crisp jeans, and a stylish blazer that travels well and also mixes with other outfits on the trip.

Not to ignore women business travelers, Omar's wife Leslie is also his business partner. While Armani and Brioni have wonderful business clothes for women, there are often other options worth exploring that may be distinctive to your own neighborhood. For example, Leslie patronizes Dara Lamb (<www.daralamb.com>), just around the corner from where Leslie and Omar live in New York. Dara tailors, among other things, a traveler's wardrobe for women—essentially an elegant three-piece suit with select separates that travel well, look stylish, and can fit into a compact bag.

At the other end of the spectrum, Leslie and Omar both have used tailors in Bangkok and Hong Kong who can produce in

24 to 48 hours some highly presentable and versatile outfits better suited for those climates (you have to be discerning though; you will find the range in these markets runs from deluxe to deplorable).

Emotionally, the better you feel, the better you perform, and that's never more true than during the stress and time changes of international travel.

Vignette

Alan was traveling on a 17-hour flight to Sydney out of Los Angeles, which was about to depart. At the last minute, the singer Dolly Parton took the seat across the aisle. She smiled, and it was clear that her road crew had occupied most of the rest of first class.

During the flight they chatted, and she was much more interested in his work than she was in telling him about hers.

Storms forced the plane to divert to Christchurch, New Zealand, which didn't have the necessary facilities to handle a packed 747. Almost everyone disembarked to visit what was available in the airport, but Alan and Dolly stayed on board and continued to chat.

Finally, four hours late, the flight arrived in Sydney. Just before landing, Dolly visited the restroom and emerged with fresh makeup and her hair perfectly arrayed. As she and Alan walked through immigration and customs, Dolly told him it had been lovely speaking with him, then turned to face a few dozen reporters and photographers, looking like a million dollars. She even looked fresher and more vibrant than anyone who had been waiting for her.

That's an entrance, and that's how you travel across borders!

---

17. Use local support and help

Make sure you have sufficient credit cards (and credit limits), and cash to purchase things locally when needed. You might need a blouse, a dentist, more appropriate local attire,[6] writing implements, computer batteries, and so forth.

Remember that you should also provide gratuities consistent with the local culture, and it's *always* important to take care of the concierges,[7] who can provide vital products and services rapidly and reliably, from play tickets to limos. Although there are always international emergency numbers for help, it's often quicker and more effective to find local help and support.

"Time" can be an oppressive jailor or benevolent enabler when you travel across borders. Trade on the infrastructure, technology, allies, and your own personal acuity to maximize productivity, pleasure, and business results, *which are synergistic, not mutually exclusive!*

One more tip: Make sure you read about the history and culture of the country you are visiting. Learn about its form of government, population, main products and services, most popular pastimes, and so forth. Learn some basic phrases. ("Where is the restroom?" doesn't hurt.) Don't enter a country as you would a strange house. Learn the layout in advance.

Vignette

Omar's friend Ron Kaufman and his Australia-born wife Jen were in Saudi Arabia to provide their customer service "college" to a leading hospital group there. Although we hear of the extremism and evident challenges facing that society, there are also pockets of corporate excellence, and impressive individual leaders trying to pave progressive alternatives. Although we all have to make our own choices of where we wish to travel, there is certainly viable consulting business to be had there.

But when you board a flight from Saudi heading home to more relaxed parts of the world, a fascinating phenomenon takes place. Saudis, particularly Saudi women, come on board dressed in full traditional garb, covered virtually from head to foot.

As the plane takes off, there is almost a scrimmage to get to the bathroom. From the bathroom emerge these same women now in form-fitting Dior dresses, perfumed and coiffed, with all the accompaniments.

So beware of judging a book by its cover, and be ready for the fact that sometimes an equivalent of a Clark Kent to Superman (or vice versa) telephone booth "transformation" may be called for, depending on where you are or where you're going.

World tour

- You can prepare your comfort when you travel and avoid surprises.

- Clients and prospects aren't impressed by torturous journeys, but by well-rested expertise.

- There is usually a plethora of local support and service you can access if you know how to ask and seek them out.

- Your image is vital, to you and to others, no more so than when far from home.

- Technology can keep you in touch and in tune with the times.

Endnotes

1. This was the famous and totally memorable opening for ABC Television's Wide World of Sports, one of the first televised shows to use emerging technology for live coverage of international events.
2. We advise you to buy gifts early in your travels, because they become distracting if you're under a deadline to buy them and meetings are running late, or you decide to return home early. You can always have the hotel business center ship gifts home for you.
3. Caution: Use your iPhone as a phone, but not to access the Web when you travel, because the latter is inefficient *and* very expensive. This will also exhaust the batteries more quickly. Thankfully, there is a setting on the iPhone to prevent it from even accidentally trying to access the Internet.
4. Some clubs will allow you into their first-class lounge if you're holding such a ticket, without membership in the airline club. But this is not always true. There are often similar provisions for business class.
5. It is highly recommended that you provide access to your general business email account to your assistant, but maintain a separate, private one for sensitive matters for you alone.
6. Alan traveled to Kuala Lumpur for the first time some years ago, and realized that the humidity would kill him if he didn't acquire lighter, more sensible clothing immediately.
7. The word, concierge, is pronounced "con-see-urzsh," not "con-see-air," and it's often mispronounced by people who occupy the job in the U.S. It's a French term, so get it right if you're going to use it.

Chapter 5

Requisites for Success: Personal

Educating yourself

As we gear up for global consulting, we certainly need to be well tooled and skilled personally, and even more than that—we need to educate ourselves continually.

Education runs deeper than skills, and gives us the heft, the gravitas, and the standing to project our expertise, to win trust, and to inspire attention—anywhere around the world. Education also suggests ongoing curiosity and a degree of immersion. Superficiality is a dangerous traveling companion.

Eminent author, Vladimir Nabokov, giving his famous lectures on literature at Columbia University, once opined that literature, indeed all art, has to be appreciated not just with our minds, but also with our spinal cords. He suggested that you know you are in the presence of artistic excellence when you experience that warm, tell-tale tingle in that "wick of humanity" called the spine. Nabokov said that if we lose our capacity to experience this, we had best just revert to zap guns and comic books because civilization will then be too heady for us.

We believe there is a takeaway there for consultants wishing to establish global success. We are not suggesting that we are going to evoke spinal rapture in our clients, and rise to the level of literature for them. What we do with our clients has to work for them first and foremost. But to deliver that, we have to offer more than glib dropdown menus or populist platitudes. We have to offer something more enduring, more genuinely insightful, perhaps even more aesthetically appealing (people do not live by efficiency alone) than the dull analytics of the run-of-the-mill, leaden consultant or the mindless buoyancy offered by the local motivator-in-chief.

Equally, for us to deliver value, we have to understand who we are helping; also how to be personally effective and functional miles away from home when need be; and we have to know the country, cultural and business realities against which our advice is to be implemented. We have to dust off our own thinking (William James, the father of clinical psychology, once suggested that most people think they are thinking when they are really only rearranging their prejudices), perhaps our own "spinal cord," and make sure we are ready both to learn about and to appreciate the world in which we hope to expand our business and our success.

Education basics: Before advising others, let's teach ourselves how to get things done

First, we have to be adept at dealing with the infrastructure that allows us to function across borders and boundaries. We have to be educated on how best to deploy existing technology, select hotels, be savvy about airports, and avail ourselves of travel support that can allow us to focus on delivering client value and not how to clear customs in time.

Many airlines set up alerts that let you know when flights are late. Some airlines are good at this, others deplorable. Flightstats.com is a service you can easily sign up for. When Omar had to make it from Shenzhen to Dubai via Beijing one evening (flights from Shenzhen are notorious for being late), and knowing that he might need a hotel in Beijing if the flight connection was missed, and that he would need reservations on the next flight out in the morning as well if so, Omar had flight-stats.com send updates to his cell phone (it will also send you emails to a web address if you prefer). That allowed him to verify that the flight was on the ground, still scheduled on time, so he could release his hotel and alternative flight booking.

Fascinatingly, his clients who had to fly to Beijing as well kept check-
ing in with Omar for updates!

Another excellent service to have on hand is OAG (Official
Airline Guide). You can get this in a physical book format, or easily
online at <www.oagflights.com>. It is a listing of flight connections
all over the world. This lets you find alternative routes, and create
your own ideal itineraries, so you aren't held hostage by the often
lackluster intuitions and caprices of a travel agent who doesn't look
far enough afield to find you what you're really after.

After all these years and all these electronics, Alan still has a physical copy of the OAG, because it's useful when an Internet connection is impossible, and even includes train service in some major
urban areas. Be aware also that a good hotel concierge will arrange
for tracking times, printing out boarding passes, and so forth.

Therefore, hotels are also something worth researching, and
you should not make assumptions about sheer functionality.
Omar once promised an analysis to a client while en route to
Japan. He expected to complete it in the next few days. The session he was facilitating was at the Sheraton Disneyland Hotel outside Tokyo. Omar was flabbergasted to learn that it had no Internet
connection in the rooms and no wi-fi access! That this was so in
Japan, arguably the most technologically advanced society on
Earth, was extraordinary. They also had only one computer in the
business center, and it was only available from 9 a.m. to
8 p.m. Not surprisingly, the line for it was around the block!
When Omar queried the manager, he said, "Disneyland Hotel is
intended for families and children." Omar asked what planet
these children came from, and whether their parents ever had to
be in touch with the outside world.

Anyway, lesson learned: When you're off the beaten track at
all, check carefully what's available and what's not.

Also, Internet service frequently doesn't work as planned due
to technical problems, storms, and plagues of locusts. In the
Caribbean, Alan has learned to find, as a backup, postal and
shipping stores, which usually offer ethernet, wi-fi, and Fedex
services in one handy location.

When you travel to places you visit too infrequently to domes-
ticate a hotel, or at times for work to small towns where you may
be staying in charming but eclectic inns, make sure that you

educate yourself about where you'll be staying ahead of time: Internet, electrical outlets, days of laundry service (particularly if you're traveling light), check-in and checkout time, proximity to the airport, and so on. (There are combination electrical adapters that can be thrown in your carry-on bag and work on every known configuration, including static electricity.)

Some minutes invested on this front can save you hours of unnecessary frustration later.

For those making long-distance calls frequently, it behooves us to be on Skype. This bit of free downloadable software has a beguiling mission statement: "To eliminate long distance." It's not there yet, but seems to be on the way. You do need a headphone with microphone, but other than that you can call free (other Skype customers) or for a relatively nominal cost (normal phones and cell phones). If you have many client, coaching, or family calls to make when on the road, this makes eminent sense.

Global learning

We advise clients on how to make their lives legitimately easier and better. "Physician heal thyself!" Let's do the same for ourselves.

Educating ourselves about technology can also pay off in other ways. Omar was asked to deliver a session for Mead Johnson. The problem was that it needed him in Hong Kong to do a keynote the day before he was committed to be in Sri Lanka. The economic buyer definitely wanted Omar's input, so here's what they came up with. When passing through Dubai, Omar would video a 45-minute keynote in three segments. The video company was identified by the client's Dubai office, and was told how to produce the video. On the day of the session, Omar's client in Sri Lanka agreed to set up a video link so that Omar could be "present" for Q&A in real time for the Hong Kong audience after each of the segments was played.

The session was a hit, and Omar delivered in Hong Kong while physically being in Colombo, Sri Lanka, thanks in part to having passed through Dubai! When it's your ideas and insights people are after, technology can be a great leveler and amplifier.

Another area we have to educate ourselves in is airport realities and possible facilities.

Again, this may be less relevant in North America, but for international travel, it helps to be educated about your options and the implications of where you are landing.

For example:

- Until recently, Heathrow had a one-bag carry-on policy, being virtually unique among major global airports in this regard. So if you boarded the plane somewhere else with two bags, say a rolling bag and a laptop or purse, and transited through Heathrow, you had to check one of them in. To avoid this lunacy, many of us started going through Frankfurt or Zurich. In part due to the uproar and lost revenue, Heathrow and virtually all the other U.K. airports have now relented, and returned to being consistent with other global airports. Flying Virgin Atlantic, during this unfortunate period, however, turned up very helpful personnel who combined several bags into a "super bag"!
- There is a "Superior Travelers" (this is its business name) program you can use when landing in airports in China (which can be a nightmare otherwise). You sign up, buy credit, and are met at the gate, taken through diplomatic channels for immigration, helped with bags, and provided with a car if you ask for one, or escorted to your own transportation otherwise. Using this program is one of the primary ways Omar made that tight connection in Beijing and got to Dubai on time.
- Passing through the U.K. often, you might sign up for the IRIS program. Frequent travelers through the U.K. can volunteer to share some background information, have their retinas scanned, and on future visits, pass through an iris scan machine without standing in any line or dealing with any immigration officer. There are airlines that provide a "fast pass" or "fast track" through immigration; Virgin Atlantic again winning praise here. (In Heathrow, you depart with it by actually bypassing traditional security and immigration, and using its private facilities, which require about 60 seconds.)
- Traveling through Hong Kong three or more times a year, you can similarly sign up for a frequent traveler program that allows you to pass through a designated and separate automated security channel.
- A similar system has been set up for frequent travelers between Canada and the U.S. as well, allowing for fast and expedient border crossing.

- Tokyo's Narita airport is roughly two-and-a-half hours by car on weekdays from Tokyo itself. On a weekend, it can be as little as a 60-minute ride. However, the Narita Express, like the Gatwick Express (Gatwick is also about two hours outside London), can get you to your destination in about 30 minutes.
- When multiple flights land in Ho Chi Minh City, immigration can take well over an hour, which can make planning a meeting or even some recreation problematic. However, you can arrange through client companies to be met (for a fee) by a "handler" (about US$50), and he provides "unofficially" the same service that is provided "officially" in China by Superior Travelers.
- Stay at the Peninsula Hotel in Hong Kong, and once the hotel Rolls drops you off at the airport, a hotel manager in a morning coat will wait in line for you taking care of required documentation.

Again, the key point is it greatly helps us to learn about airports, gates, distance from the city, tips about immigration, to check for VIP services (sometimes when you have to make a commitment and time is tight, these aren't luxuries at all), and anything that can make your landings or takeoffs as stress-free as possible. That way, your confidence is bolstered, and your energy is preserved for the job at hand.

This is particularly important if you catch the bug, and start traveling regularly for business. Even if you travel more occasionally, this education will liberate your time and energy so they can be better deployed.

Educating yourself for success: Understanding countries and people

The preceding is tactical, and now we turn to the more substantive. It is hard to proffer advice or to partner effectively when we are ignorant of the realities people face and some of the local or regional challenges that give rise to the issues they are asking for help with.

Omar was contacted by Nestlé of Russia for help in strengthening the communication effectiveness of the senior team with each other and with their next-level leaders. As Omar explored this with the CEO, he asked whether the transition Russia has been in the midst of since the collapse of the Berlin Wall had created any unusual organizational dynamics.

The question released a gusher of input from the CEO and his team. One key factor he cited is that people in Russia had been raised to have loyalty to the state and the cliques to which they belonged and relied on for survival. Although things had moved on pragmatically, psychologically these were the same people who had been conditioned in that way, and company and team loyalty were novel concepts that would have to evolve. We couldn't therefore count on them as something the employees of Nestlé Russia would intuitively understand and find naturally compelling. Without having learned this, there would have been no way to design an approach that could truly help this leadership team.

Many expatriate managers sent to China similarly are ready to rend their garments in despair. One of Omar's coachees there said he was at a loss because English skills were limited. The few Chinese managers who were bilingual and foreign educated were in heavy demand, and there was a bidding war for them. Those who weren't foreign educated, but could speak functional English and had picked up management skills locally had a very difficult time with ambiguity. They wanted precise instructions. Asking for their judgment and initiative often paralyzed them. Their lives within their society had not rewarded risk taking or expressing what seemed to them like wanton individuality.

Again, a nation and society in transition, but understanding the centrifugal and centripetal forces at play is crucial to coaching both the expatriates who are in the eye of this storm, and also to working with these Chinese managers who are devotedly working on evolving a larger and more holistic skill-set.

Alan was given a crash course on arriving in Quito in why he should not approach or trust the local police, learning that many didn't have guns or bullets, and had to extort money to buy them (which made them even more effective at extortion). In Colombia, he was advised never to travel into the countryside, and turned down a very lucrative proposal that would have put him squarely in harm's way. ("Don't worry, the Mercedes is armored and can withstand light mines.")

We can hardly be global consultants and not be fascinated by these trends, realities and even pressures. Our job is not to despair or to rail at these aspects, but to help our clients find the right way to ignite positive change.

We think it is a wasteful shame when inaccurate stereotypes are foisted on us as permanent assumptions about people. This is far less helpful than understanding the evolving realities that may temporarily or otherwise push people in certain directions.

Many people tell us the Japanese, due to their educational system, are not innovative. This runs smack into the extraordinary product innovation shown by Japan in many sectors. In its heyday, Akio Morita transformed Sony, for example, into a highly creative, nonhierarchical work environment. Delving deeper, we discover that you have to balance innovation and pragmatism in attempting to understand Japan.

Alan was told that the Japanese would not participate in small-group discussions and focus groups, to avoid embarrassment. But they were happy to do so when a "reporter" was named to give the consensus of the group without requiring each person to stake out his or her position personally.

When Omar lived in Japan (his father was posted to Tokyo as an ambassador), next to his home were a *Shinto* shrine and temple. *Shinto* was once the state religion of Japan. It has affinities with Taoism, and is focused on the spiritual in nature. When Japan ceased to have a state religion, funds for shrines such as this one were cut. To survive, the monks converted the front of the temple into a parking lot—much needed in that neighborhood! By day the monks parked cars, in the evening they repaired to their meditation and worship. Visiting the shrine, one is struck by how beautifully they have maintained its beauty and traditional classicism inside, while outside, a bustling parking lot is operated with pragmatic efficiency!

Global learning

People in other cultures are often both more and less than they seem. Our job is to be students of reality, not purveyors of myths.

When this story and its insight are shared with Japanese clients, they almost invariably light up with appreciation. This has often relaxed them to share other issues, challenges, and realities they may want help with.

It is also helpful to have facts. It is a staple of economic conventional wisdom among many in the U.S. that Europe, by having more social welfare, has correspondingly high unemployment.

This is certainly true for France and Germany. But Denmark and the Netherlands, for example, have roughly the same unemployment rate as we do in the U.S., while Switzerland and Austria have lower rates. Similarly, the U.S. is inundated with stories of the high quality of life in Scandinavia. Yet these countries also the highest have suicide rates in the world. So if we flash statistics we haven't bothered to check or study, we have a hard time coming across as credible. After all, a client may wonder what other assumptions and facts we haven't checked!

Omar was visiting his local wine merchants in New York, and someone overheard that he was traveling to Singapore. "My God, be careful, that's not safe!" Omar was shocked, because Singapore is certainly one of the safest cities on the planet. Of course, when Omar tells this story overseas, people chuckle and say, "And this from a New Yorker!" Omar then has to provide a reality check in the other direction, pointing out that the crime rate in New York has plummeted in recent years, and it is now one of the very safest urban centers in the U.S.

Experience varies, but we've found that it's safer in a back alley in Hong Kong than a main street in Rio de Janeiro, and much safer in a tiny square in Buenos Aires at night than on the main highway leading to Mexico City in broad daylight.

Many people think of Bangladesh as one of the poorest countries in the world, buffeted by disasters and emotional and political turmoil. Much of that is true. However, for that neighborhood of South Asia, it has an impressive growth rate, local companies that are highly professional and doing well regionally, and global success stories such as Muhammad Yunus (a local hero there), who is now a Nobel laureate for his pioneering work in micro-enterprise (he is the founder of Grameen Bank). Knowing some of this is clearly important in forging relationships there, having stimulating and sensible exchanges, and being fit to consult for those who live and work in that country, and are also likely proud of their progress, as well as being often disgruntled by their recurring challenges.

In working with a Saudi client who was saying that a diverse workforce for them was a global mandate, but a challenge culturally because of their Islamic roots, Omar was able to challenge this by pointing out that early Islamic tradition made room for other faiths. Omar cited how when he was in Spain for Unilever's global finance team, the Spanish travel company they were working with mentioned that Muslim-influenced Spanish towns such as Cordoba (which houses arguably one of the most architecturally stunning mosques, if not buildings, in the world) are still revered by Spaniards, because it reminds them of a golden age under Muslim rule, when Muslims, Christians, and Jews co-existed in relative harmony. They realize that many disparities still existed, and Christians and Jews weren't treated as equals. But that Spanish travel executive reminded Omar that it was a period when people of multiple faiths could flourish together. That was ended not by Islamic fanatics, but by Ferdinand, Isabella and the Inquisition.

When the Saudi client heard this Spanish "take" on aspects of Islamic history, he stopped and spoke almost wistfully to Omar: "You're right; those early Muslims built a civilization; they worked with others. They built cities, and advanced science and math. That's our real tradition, or should be." This Saudi finance company moved on from this imagined impasse.

When people debate the most beautiful cities in the world, the most common candidates seem to be Sydney, Cape Town, and Rio. In Cape Town, conducting a Leadership Journey, it helped for Omar to know the deep and abiding poignance for South Africans of Robben Island, where Mandela was incarcerated for 17 years; or the bittersweet challenge of the many enterprising townships, where poverty and HIV are still such current challenges; to the intoxicatingly beautiful Provence-like landscape of the neighboring wineries, and the marvelous cuisine abounds there. These are all aspects of the experience of Cape Town and South Africa, and not to be aware of these, or to be able to tap into them, renders us far too oblivious to the people, their passions, and perhaps the paradigms we either have to help them take advantage of or to help them to transcend.

The great harbors of the world are probably Sydney, San Francisco, New York, and Hong Kong. Alan sat on a veranda overlooking Repulse Bay in Hong Kong, sharing its history with a local client, who was impressed that they shared such an intimate knowledge of the building of the great city. A treat in Sydney, on the balcony of the Intercontinental over breakfast, was pointing out to an Australian client that while he was right about the great power of being descended from prisoners, he had the U.S. to thank because, after 1776, the British could no longer send the inmates to America!

So let's educate ourselves about where we are going. More than just the local mores that we spoke of earlier, let's also learn about the history, culture, economy, challenges, and opportunities. We don't have to be experts in each, but we need to know enough to be able to engage with alertness and awareness. We can hardly consult effectively otherwise.

Wonderful technique: Print out a few pages about currency, crops, history, culture, heroes, and so forth, and carry them in your briefcase to read on the plane and review just before key meetings.

The great Jewish teacher, Rabbi Hillel, was allegedly challenged by someone to distill the Torah into one sentence. This whimsical interlocutor said, "If you can summarize the Torah in a sentence while balancing on one leg, I'll convert."

Rising to the challenge, Rabbi Hillel is said to have not only balanced on one leg, but also responded with spellbinding simplicity in what is a clear precursor of the Golden Rule: "Whatever you would not want done to you, do not do unto others. That is the whole of the Torah, the rest is commentary."

Well, you and I would not enjoy being advised on intimate and crucial matters to us and our business by someone willfully ignorant about us, our nation, our society, our realities, and our culture. Neither does anyone else.

Educating yourself for life: Lifelong learning

Most people would concede that we live in a high-tech world. However, in high-tech times, "high-touch" has never been more important. Of all the prognosticators, John Naisbitt was one of the best, being prescient about this 30 years ago.

As we need fewer physical interactions whether we are halfway across the world or just across town, when we do interact in person, those interactions mean a lot more, and carry that much more potential significance.

Part of people wanting you in their ambit, whether as a resource whose blog they eagerly read, or a coach they want to call, or someone they want to invite to spend a day with them and their team, will depend on how much of an object of interest and stimulus you are, over and above your published expertise. It is our savvy, our insight, our take on life, our point of view that help to establish a personal brand and to create the distinctiveness that sets us apart from the passing trade.

So lifelong personal education, not necessarily targeted at a particular utility or professional relevance, helps create a foundation for being genuinely fascinating and not just functionally proficient.

An entrepreneur friend, John MacDonald, told us of how he selected someone to represent his interests in the Netherlands. He interviewed two candidates for country manager. He sent both for a visit to Amsterdam, Rotterdam, and the Hague. Both presented sensible, compelling business plans for what they would do if given the role.

However, when asked what he thought of the country, the first one pooh-poohed that aspect, saying he hadn't had time to "sightsee." Probed further, he complained about unfriendly locals, bleak weather, and odd food.

Global learning

Assuming strong expertise, the more interesting and stimulating you are, the more naturally people will be attracted to working with you. We select our favorite restaurants, cafes, and perhaps even hotels in part based on where we enjoy hanging out. Why should our clients not differentiate on the basis of who they want to hang out with either?

The second candidate beamed with delight, sharing the warm hospitality he had enjoyed (no, the Dutch don't flash megawatt smiles at first encounter, but are very amiable and open to dialog), the wonderful cheese, herring, chocolates and aromatic coffee he had enjoyed, the social compassion of a country that puts Braille on their currency, the richness of art housed at the Van Gogh museum and Rijksmuseum, and more. It wasn't hard for John to select the candidate who would be happier with the assignment, who his Dutch clients and team members would prefer to work with, and who would likely have the perspicacity to understand the country, society, and even economy where he would be seeking to add value.

Years ago, Omar was at a Japanese celebration and was taught "*Tanko-Bushi*," the ancient coal-mining dance. It is a hoot, and to Western perception, is very amusing. However, the Japanese found Omar's rendition of it to be even more amusing!

To this day, Omar's fondness for this coal-mining dance and his (inadvertently) rather amusing performance of it provides a fascinating open sesame for conversations in Japan with bankers, executives, professors, ambassadors, and more. For example, the Japanese ambassador in Singapore asked Omar over for a "demo." He promised to prepare a feast of *sushi, sashimi,* and *tempura* to fuel the effort. When Omar learned the dance, it was simply for fun. He had no idea he was picking up something so venerable in its own way. You never do know...

We are strong advocates of eating locally, understanding what we're eating, and commenting intelligently about it (at least before the sixth *sake*). Alan has downed tripe (*menudo*) in Mexico City at midnight out of earthen pots, and once ate the national dish of Chile in an undistinguished airport restaurant, over the loud protestations of his local alliance partner, who informed him that even the Chileans would not try such a thing.

In a similar vein, if heading over to see *The Nutcracker* in New York over Christmas, it helps to know that the New York Ballet puts on George Balanchine's version, which was a turning point in dance in America from the time it was first staged in 1954. But other companies, such as the San Francisco Ballet, have their own versions (the San Francisco Ballet was the first to introduce Tchaikovsky's classic to the U.S., even though it was the Balanchine version that established it firmly as a seasonal classic).

Why know this? That is because it heightens our appreciation of whichever version we are seeing, it lets us be aware of the tradition we are participating in, and it adds to our enjoyment of the ballet and our sense of occasion. All of these are aptitudes and faculties, that honed overall in life, add to our capacity to engage with and savor many aspects of the world around us. These are also good ingredients for success in consulting globally, or indeed for virtually any other field in which who we are, not just what we know, matters.

Global learning

As Peter Drucker reminded us, ongoing adult re-education will increasingly influence the competitiveness of nations—so too individuals!

Nor are we encouraging experiencing only classical Western examples of cultural taste. In Hanoi, the water puppet theater is marvelous; in Sri Lanka, Kandyan dancing is wonderfully rhythmic and evocative; *Mardi Gras*, whether enjoyed in Rio or Venice or New Orleans ("Fat Tuesday" literally in French, the final day of Carnival—the three days before Ash Wednesday leading to Lent) can be life-affirming merriment; the passionate rock art and bark paintings give powerful insight into the traditions and genius of Australian aboriginal art; and so on.

Moreover, don't be limited by belief systems or lack of belief systems. St. Peter's in the Vatican, the great reclining Buddha in Bangkok, Mt. St. Michel in France, the Wailing Wall in Jerusalem, and scores of other religious sites are hugely rewarding for artistry, history, spirituality, and understanding.

Not only is such education personally edifying and challenging to our paradigms, perceptions, and insights, there is also nothing more flattering to people than to let them teach you something. Being open to learning about them, their society, and their culture, what matters to them is the most credible way to build rapport, convey a real commitment to partnering with them and adding value for them.

Sometimes, a bit of cultural translation helps. Omar was working with a global Johnson & Johnson team, and someone kept saying, "We mustn't act like Pollyanna here," referring to the indestructible optimism associated with the literary character, Pollyanna. One of the team leaders, a Frenchman, was befuddled. "What do you mean, Pollyanna?" he whispered to Omar, wanting to preserve face. Happily, Omar (thanks in part to a prescient high-school teacher who had introduced this classic to Omar's class) was able to reply, "An equivalent would be Pangloss in Voltaire's *Candide*." A knowing smile came over the French team leader's face; he gave Omar a grateful nod, and dove into the conversation.

Keeping abreast of interesting books is also part of what doing business involves in a role in which people look to us for advice and judgment. We have readily delved into the provocative book *Black Swan* (by Nassim Taleb), which argues that many large-scale events are unpredictable, and are triggered by unexpected, seemingly peripheral events. Many thoughtful people are intrigued by what this implies for predictions in everything from the stockmarket to global politics. Not to be aware of an idea like this, which many globally are keen to discuss or learn about, is to some extent, to be asleep at the wheel.

We use this book as an example; there are many out there. Which ones you delve into matters less than that you frequently stay aware of what's justifiably grabbing attention locally and internationally, not only in terms of world events, but in terms of ideas, trends, tastes, and technologies.

Educating habits: Global credibility

Different countries and cultures invariably have different habits, intuitions, and reflexes. But we've found from benchmarking successful and effective individuals around the world, nine habits that are constants that we have to inculcate in ourselves, encourage in our allies, and display reliably.

1. Be on time. (Except where you're not supposed to be, as in Latin America.) Enough said. This trumps everything else. Perhaps even better: Conform to time expectations.
2. If you say it, do it. Brands, trust, credibility, all live or die on the basis of what we do once we've committed to something.
3. Follow through. Starting things isn't enough; completing them, getting them done is what matters.
4. Be professional, courteous, and generous. Nobody enjoys amateurism, rudeness, or stinginess.
5. Ask, don't assume. Check facts, check assumptions, ask for what you need, be willing to hear "no." Dispel illusions, and ask better questions that ignite positive cooperation.
6. Be coachable. If you're unwilling to be corrected, not amenable to learning, averse to listening, hostile to adaptation, you can hardly or credibly ask for these aptitudes from your clients.

Global learning

Successes and failures have two major things in common: habits and discipline!

7. Accept responsibility; be accountable. The buck stops with us. We don't whine; we face reality early; and through our initiative, we then transform it whenever possible and make the most of it gracefully when we can do nothing about it. This is as important in our projects as in everything else.
8. Do a little more than is expected. Provide some value-added service or input, be a bit more ardent and attentive in ensuring that the agreed results are realized, and display caring and commitment by exceeding what is minimally expected. This is

both about our own esteem and professional pride and our investment in the relationship we're here to forge.

9. Don't be even an inadvertent chauvinist. Don't condemn a bullfight in Torremolinos without understanding its genesis and cultural bulwarks. Don't dismiss *kabuki* because you can't understand what seems like shouting. Cultural artifacts don't spring up overnight. They are the results of generations of adaptation.

Educating ourselves in these habits and then living them will make us credible, referable, and a class act anywhere in the world.

World tour

- We have to educate ourselves to avail ourselves of technology, tools, and services that can preserve our energy, our time, our focus, and at times our peace of mind as we get things done.

- The deeper our education in the countries and cultures that are our intended markets, the more applicable our expertise and insight become.

- Developing and demonstrating the capacity to learn about the world at large stimulates both our critical and appreciative faculties, each of which can add so much to consulting success.

- Building habits and discipline that increase reliability frees us from battling ourselves to do the right things. As those personal examples of credibility happen "naturally," we are enabled to make the degree of impact we should want to.

Chapter 6

Requisites for Success: New Paradigms

Creating global value

Once we're equipped and ready to make good use of technology, to travel in a savvy manner, and to educate ourselves so that we can be both stimulating and pertinent in many locales, it is critical to find ways of converting our latent wisdom, expertise, and insight into increasingly marketable value.

Many times, a need crystallizes as we build a trusting relationship with a key economic buyer. But many times people come to us and are drawn to us because of offerings we have created. The packaging of our intellectual capital in ways that drives interest and creates demand is a primary way in which we can consult globally, often without traveling very far. When we do travel, this ensures that the return on time and energy is almost as exciting as the trip can be.

We spoke earlier about the dangers of commoditization. When we create an offering, an approach, a session, a way to convey value that is distinctively branded and imaginatively communicated, and creates a fanbase of enthusiasts, we effectively and often dramatically distinguish ourselves from the hoi polloi of consultants still peddling generics such as "meeting facilitation," "team building," or "wellness."

Compare "meeting facilitation" with the value speaking expert (and our colleague) Patricia Fripp provides in helping leaders to make a powerful communication impact, or "team building" with the Leadership Journeys we've described earlier, run by Omar and his team, or "wellness" with a potent few days spent with Alan on his "Renaissance Journey," which targets leading a remarkable life.

If how we convey our expertise doesn't display in various parts our imagination, our creativity, our insight, and perhaps even our zeal, why should anyone believe us when we tell them we have these in abundant supply if they would only tap them?

Such value conveyed globally is a primary way to strengthen an international brand, and to make our business vastly more profitable at the same time.

Creating new value

Many times clients have somewhat imprecise needs, and the value they seek is the difference they believe we can add by simply being there. For example, why should any client call us around the world to attend a meeting? However, Omar coaches a global Unilever leader, in charge of a €5 billion segment of Unilever's business worldwide. As he transitioned from a regional to a global job, this leader wanted Omar to attend its global conference, to immerse himself in its challenges, to meet key people he may later support, and to facilitate an afternoon's session. For this, Omar was flown business class to Phuket (the best class available on the route at the time), put up in a top resort where the meeting was being held, and paid US$30,000 for these three days, in which his "active" input (as in running a session) was sought for about two hours.

However, such a deep and abiding coaching relationship had been built that this leader, embarking on a larger role, valued Omar's input, insights, and engagement enough to ask for what was essentially his active presence. In this sense, Omar could hardly start marketing "conference attendance" as a value to other clients. However, build the quality and depth of relationships with the right leaders, and the range of what they find genuinely valuable in interacting with you can be positively astonishing. For this to work, we have to have already demonstrated the value of our observations and insights on many occasions, and communicated them to our clients in a way that provides tangible benefits and valued guidance.

Alan is a contrarian *par excellence*. One of the ways he quickly caught people's attention is by taking the hobby horses of the day and challenging them. At the height of the Total Quality craze, Alan would write an article suggesting that Total Quality programs hurt actual quality! Most who have heard this argument agree it was not just shock therapy—it was a lucid and penetrating analysis. Namely, the bureaucracy of TQM programs created an inward-looking obsession for companies, who then didn't look outward at customers, or markets, or toward delivering real value. They were trying to conform to the "specs" of the program.

At that time, a continent or two away, Omar found a valuable niche by going to companies such as Engro (an ex-Exxon subsidiary and at that time, one of the most successful employee buyouts in history) and the then Reckitt & Coleman (now Reckitt Benckiser) to help them to resuscitate the original intent behind their quality programs. They were usually very keen for such help once they found the bureaucratic rollout sold to them by some "methodology" consultant to be onerous, oppressive, and counterproductive in practice.

With the slogan of continuous improvement, from the Japanese *kaizen*, Omar and his company Sensei focused instead with these companies on catalyzing the attitude of creating small ongoing improvements that mattered to customers and the market, inculcating the behavior needed for productive interdepartmental collaboration. They explored communication breakdowns, challenged poor listening to customers (external and internal), encouraged a better willingness to probe to the root cause of problems pragmatically, and coached the use of project teams not as window dressing, but rather to meet genuine business opportunities. In short, they took on some of the most critical things that were the bane of most backfiring quality efforts.

As a result, many companies happily invested US$200,000 with Omar to redeem their US$2,000,000 earlier investment in a "famous" program (they realized that if something weren't rescued from all this outlay, many heads would be on the chopping block!). Omar suggested to some of these clients that next time, he'd be happy to accept the US$2,000,000 himself, would create and then dismantle loads of unnecessary complexity directly, and thereby relieve them of the need to seek any additional redemption. The irony in this wry suggestion was rarely appreciated!

However, the real quality impact and value liberated *were* appreciated enough for Omar and his associates to do this work across seven countries in Southeast and South Asia over several years, very lucratively.

Key point: Don't ever underestimate the added value of your personal participation. You are the talent; the antithesis of a commodity. While we encourage remote work and diminished labor intensity, the "power of presence" is priceless.

Working for one of the largest banks in the world, Alan was told that the options of him training internal people in his concepts, or of using his alliance partners in key cities were politically unacceptable. He would have to be the one to travel through Asia and Europe to work with all senior managers so that the person and message were the same.

The bank didn't blink at the US$350,000 fee for Alan to deliver personally. Sitting in the nose of a 747, his wife, who accompanied him throughout the trip, estimated that he was actually making US$14,400 per hour, because she knew how much of each day he was actually on the client's site.

If you do the division, you'll be astonished at the total hours he "worked" for this overwhelmingly delighted client.

Global learning

Many times your next consulting windfall is right under your nose. You just have to connect what you can do to what your clients need.

The point here is that we certainly first have to create value by building powerful relationships and offering value that becomes ever more unique because it is anchored in that distinctive relationship. But, additionally, we can create value by looking at the real needs underlying the transient fads that flit across the consulting horizon. Usually, there is a kernel of real need lurking beneath the froth of whatever is being ladled out by the large consulting shops and by jargon merchants. If we can meet that need in a way that is consistent with our brand, experience, and expertise, we can create exciting new revenue streams. If that approach, like Omar's "Living Quality" brand in those days, captures a common need, you'll be invited to replicate what you can offer, not only at home, but very likely in many geographies and ports of call.

Make sure you know what you've got

Sometimes we have potential expertise, but don't realize how it could be parlayed into a valuable and lucrative offering. While at Oxford, Omar had trained as a crisis counselor, and had helped run the Oxford crisis counseling service, Nightline. Subsequently, Omar worked with some of the founders of neurolinguistic programming (NLP), a form of behavioral psychology. As a result, his consulting was naturally laced with a coaching approach

However, this was before the mass proliferation of "coaching" as a management phenomenon. Two stimuli led to Omar creating a distinctive approach that has been sought globally in this value space.

The first was when he was presenting a session for the American Society of Training and Development (ASTD). In the audience was the president of Motorola University (their internal knowledge-management institute). "You should be a coach," he told Omar. Although at the time this was a relatively novel idea, the sheer logic of providing leaders, particularly globetrotting ones away from their homes and other support structures, with a confidential sounding board—a peer with no other agenda than their success—seemed truly compelling.

But Omar still didn't know how to package or offer that distinctively enough so that people would seek him or his company out in particular.

The second piece of the puzzle fell into place a year later in Singapore, where Steve Morris, an accomplished coach, was putting together change packages for key Singaporean companies and even government ministries (the National Library Board had used about half a million dollars of coaching input from Steve's company!).

About six months later, Omar launched "The Coaching Breakthrough," his company Sensei's approach to growing leaders and fast-tracking the development of high potentials.

It came about when the regional director for Asia Pacific for British American Tobacco (BAT), Patrick, asked him how BAT could help their Asian leaders to get past the "glass ceiling", keeping them from reaching certain echelons of leadership. Thirty-two leaders were identified, and Patrick and Omar figured that if even 20 percent of them in the next three years were able to move into more senior positions, so that a European expatriate wouldn't be needed, that would be roughly US$1 million per position (taking into account relocation costs, the full expatriate salary plus package, and so on) of benefit.

So they created an approach that involved getting feedback from BAT on what three or four key behaviors, aptitudes, and abilities would have to be consistently demonstrated by these already promising Asian leaders for them to be serious contenders for these senior roles.

Bosses were enrolled, an assessment was done of these leaders against these identified necessary capabilities, they were put through team sessions that targeted these aptitudes, and given a personal coach (two associates of Omar's) to work intensively with over nine months.

The project was very successful, and a new value offering was in hand—using coaching to fast-track the development of high potentials, combining individual coaching, team learning, and a robust partnership with their bosses, who had to be willing to acknowledge the growth taking place.

The ingredients for this were arguably present in Omar's background. But he had to look for trends (coaching), approaches (using coaching for concerted, rather than just individual, development), and client needs (to reduce the dependence on expatriates and develop local talent) to create this approach.

Once your niche is established, packaged and presented in a certain way, then truly you'll be the "global expert" in that particular approach, and will be sought for accordingly.

India is a fast-developing market. One of the challenges of consulting there, however, is that India is also an incubator for very many consultants. Their command of English is excellent; they have many developing industries to cut their teeth into; and Indian companies can be quite nationalist. So they will rarely import consulting talent when they feel they can get it locally— and truly they have more choice than most on this front.

However, no one else does Leadership Journeys in the way that Omar and his team present them. They were developed to allow clients who wanted to interact outside a sterile hotel room, but didn't want a nonsensical adventure trip in the wilderness as an alternative. Instead, by "journeying" from one place to the other, experiencing new cultures, expanding personal paradigms, and having business-critical crucial conversations along the way, they experienced something quite unique.

A group of Indian entrepreneurs who had previously worked at Unilever, and had experienced these Journeys, contacted Omar and said, "You have to come and do this for our new team in India." There was no competition and no negotiation, and the Indian team fully accepted that Omar (originally Pakistani) came from the U.S., with a support team from Sri Lanka, to conduct a Leadership Journey in India, with a local logistics company providing support.

Global learning

When you create a powerful new process, approach or experience, you may provoke your own version of Elvis impersonators, but in this domain, you'll remain "the King."

So look at your expertise, evaluate and listen to the most critical problems being faced by clients, be attentive to different ways of providing and packaging value that you come across (for example, Alan excels at this, using everything from tele-seminars, online forums, workshops, week-long colleges, CDs and DVDs, mentoring in person or by phone), and link that to your brand.

No one will go anywhere else for a Leadership Journey run the way Omar conducts them, nor will they be asking for a blurred imitation of Alan's Million Dollar Consulting College.

Clearly, we have to respond to real needs, and not wander around with "solutions looking for a problem." But when there is a clear pattern of need, we also have to *create customers*, as Peter Drucker advised. If we do it astutely, with savvy and market insight, then the movie *Field of Dreams* was right on: "Build it and they will come."

To make a global impact, build momentum

Anyone can land and run a few sessions in a foreign market. Perhaps they'll even be well received. But then what? If you really want to create a fan base and ongoing business in that market, you have to build some momentum, until people start "looking out" for what you offer.

Ron Kaufman landed in Singapore to help Singapore Airlines design a customer service curriculum. Falling in love with the Lion City, Ron stayed and created a brand around uplifting customer service. His take on "service" was upbeat, practical, imaginative, quirky, and abundant with local Asian examples, as well as global Western benchmarks.

Pretty soon, Ron's customer service sessions like "The Secrets of Superior Service" and "Partnership Power," and his very popular "Writing Back" (replying to customer complaints in written form) became a valued feature of corporate life in Singapore, both for public programs and for in-house work. It took Ron many years of landing, making an impact, tapering the presentations and understanding the challenges of adapting global standards of service to an increasingly global yet fundamentally Asian city (Singapore).

Soon, Ron was being sought in Malaysia, Thailand, the Philippines, India, Australia (where his wife is from), and more. The currently thriving emirate of Dubai benchmarks Singapore in many ways. The Dubai Quality Group asked Ron to do a "free" speech. Realizing that the workforce of Dubai is largely made up of Filipinos, Indians, Pakistanis, and Sri Lankans (many of whom Ron had addressed over several years), Ron was confident he could create the requisite impact to justify the effort.

Today, the Middle East is a highly profitable market for Ron, where he commands upward of US$18,000 a day for his customer service sessions. In those regions, if you think of uplifting your team to understand and deliver enthusiastic service, Ron will be a natural choice, and his delighted customer–advocates do most of the selling for him.

Once he knew that many companies wished they could repeat the Ron Kaufman message and experience for new inductees, or have people spend more time on the tools and concepts, he packaged his intellectual capital into a "Customer Service College." Companies now buy DVD presentations of various aspects of his approach to customer service, certified external trainers (Ron and his associates) and certified internal course leaders present the material, and the company is then licensed to use the material for building a customer service culture over time. Now, instead of just selling individual days at US$18,000 (nothing wrong with those either!), Ron sells US$250,000 to US$500,000 consulting and support packages to companies around the world.

This has become possible because he built his niche, his brand, and his delivery, created a "tipping point" of clients who had received business benefit as well as enjoying the experience, and expanded outward from a personally chosen hub (in this case, Singapore).

One learning is that by focusing on smaller markets, be they city-states such as Singapore, or countries with a specific business hub (Kuala Lumpur, Manila, Amsterdam, Sydney), you can develop some real "buzz" about what you do. You can build relationships, get to know the place, write for local papers, speak at various public events, and become known as a trusted advisor who offers distinctive benefit. Once you've done that over several targeted visits, you will naturally be recommended to neighboring markets, expanding your opportunities and amplifying the premium nature of what you do will be natural.

At the time Omar was working for Hilton in Sri Lanka, his approach to "Living Quality" (deliver quality not bureaucracy) caught on in Colombo. Although the almost perpetual civil war that has ravaged Sri Lanka occasionally flared up, in the mid-1990s to the turn of the century, Colombo was thriving. Omar was able to extensively offer the continuous improvement consulting

Global learning

Enthusiasm for something that many have experienced and benefited from is often infectious. Inculcate this in a critical mass of clients in various markets as a facet of your work, and you'll find opportunities continually headed in your direction.

we wrote about earlier in the chapter, as one leader after the other, in a relatively small and incestuous business market like Colombo's, spoke about what they had embarked upon and what they had achieved as a result. That Omar and Leslie came to know Sri Lanka quite well, and could speak from a position of cultural insight, rather than ignorance or worse, condescension, clinched the deal. Omar was able to create a local operating base that is self-supporting there to this day, and back when the market merited his direct involvement, such consulting packages brought in US$300,000 to US$400,000 each year from a relatively poor country that, nevertheless, had some very successful businesses and conglomerates operating from its shores.

Alan is able to schedule high-end workshops antipodally—in London and Sydney—merely using his brand and a few local connections from his many visits (15 to London, 10 to Sydney). He builds around those workshops, which are the "anchors," consulting, speaking, and coaching work while he is on site, and also creates alliances and develops prospects. He has already collected US$40,000 for a trip to Australia that is eight months away.

His visits are sought for and underwritten by those who consider him a periodic solution and leader.

As we've said, clearly you have to offer what is needed. But when what you offer becomes *part of the need*, you have to (if you enjoy the place and want to build repeat business there) make enough visits (they don't have to be frequent, a few times a year but with some regularity), so you can expand your base of contacts, and create enough positive ripples that in time can aggregate into significant waves of demand.

Decide how you want to deliver value

While traveling can be a wondrous thing, it is equally wondrous to travel on your own terms and be able to generate fees and profits and wealth without going very far from home—while still tapping a global market.

Alan's mentoring program is a wonderful example. Since Alan is readily contactable by phone and email, people can have more access to him when they really need him than to a conventional coach who they can see "in person," but at select intervals and at specific times.

Moreover, he is able to offer his expertise and experience to people virtually anywhere in the world. More to the point, while luxuriating at a favorite resort, or emerging from a spa treatment, he can spend an hour returning calls and replying to emails, and be done with a day's work. He will have added tremendous value, and earned a portion of the US$3,500 to US$9,500 and up (based on the package they opt for) individuals pay over six months to be mentored by Alan.

Many of Alan's signature sessions and workshops are held close to Providence, where he lives. People travel to him, and do so happily, because they can't get that input, innovation, and perspective anywhere else.

Jim Collins, author of *Good To Great* and co-author of *Built To Last*, filters out CEOs or leaders who are really serious about his consulting assistance by also requiring that they travel to him. He has found that being sought for very specific expertise and for his ongoing research into thriving companies and leaders preselects out leaders who are just "fishing," as opposed to those really committed to producing results, who therefore arrive really ready to roll up their sleeves and get on with it. Nothing is at a greater premium to a CEO than his or her time. Jim therefore asks for that first, along with the dollars that can usually be far more easily found.

Omar now can be at home for a month in New York, and coach his global clients from London, Geneva, Amsterdam, Dubai, Singapore, and Bangkok. He does this by email and telephone calls either late evening New York time or first thing in the morning. He is therefore in touch, spends roughly an hour a day on this, and still generates significant income and produces substantial value, without leaving home. In Omar's case, these are global leaders he has cultivated deep relationships with first. But he's learned to connect fast, demonstrate value, and show them that such remote access gives them the advantages of his input without the aggravations of comparing calendars, booking flights and hotels, and interfering with their busy schedules unduly. Given these benefits, the capacity to add value in this way then becomes a competitive advantage rather than a deterrent.

Ways of delivering global value are only as limited as our own imagination. Dan Taylor is an attorney by training, Dan has authored more than 60 articles and two books, and has appeared on many radio and television programs. Dan is a nationally recognized speaker on creating new and unique processes to transform the family law system in the U.S. and to influence such approaches globally.

As president of the Wealth Capital Group in Charlotte, Dan provides advisory services to help deal creatively and yet sanely with aspects of his clients' personal, business, and family lives.

Dan's business model works through a combination of helping people structure key conversations they need to have and making them aware of realities and implications that are implicit in their decisions. For example, Dan has pioneered the "Parent Care Solution," a way to have individuals help their parents make key financial decisions in concert with their family, while they still can. People sometimes avoid these conversations because of the emotions involved. However, by translating this into a series of seven-to-ten discrete, life-improving decisions that are ideally made collaboratively, Dan has created a process that empowers families and helps them strengthen their relationships as they create pragmatic foundations for the future. Now this is being looked at as a template by many global corporations as a facility they can offer employees.

His "Divorce Mediation Solution" helps those whose marriages are ending to reduce the time, expense, and impact of the divorce drastically, by helping them to identify and engage in the most critical conversations they need to have in a future-focused way. He helps them to use the legal system only to authenticate the decisions the couple has made, rather than as a way to aggravate the acrimony.

Dan's calling card is to create approaches to those personal issues that often are neglected, or are potentially divisive, and convert them into constructive, collaborative, legally and financially insightful dialogues and options, which work in the real world and produce an appreciable financial and personal impact.

Not only does he "own" these processes, which people pay a premium to learn and be coached through, but as a result people also travel *to* him from around the world now for his consultation on other vexing issues for which traditional solutions are inadequate. He co-creates a process with them that they can carry through, always requiring significant personal ownership and application, with judicious input from Dan and his team at key junctures.

Dan has therefore created a value proposition that depends on intellectual capital, not personal exhaustion. He enjoys vast discretionary time (one of our definitions of real wealth), and has built a multimillion dollar consulting and advisory practice to boot.

The real insight here is, once you've chosen how to parlay your expertise into a niche, and you've created enough of a groundswell so that people are attracted into your orbit, then judiciously combine delivery modes, so that you can balance traveling out to clients and getting people to come to you. Moreover, there are lots of good ways to do things, not just one royal road, so experiment with differ-

Global learning

Be as creative in structuring how you deliver, where you deliver, and the medium of delivery as you would be in generating client solutions.

ent ways of delivering value until you find an equation that while being highly effective for your clients, is also attractive to you, is time efficient, and produces an outstanding return-on-energy.

Make it easy

Finally, whatever modes you select, and however you package and deliver value, make yourself easy to do business with if you're going to add value globally.

This means phone numbers that actually get through to you, with either an answering service that is attended to, or a good virtual assistant, who will get the message to you promptly. This means email that is regularly attended, although not maniacally through every conversation or dinner as the zoned-out email junkies who live in their own private haze demonstrate in restaurants, bars, and lounges around the world to Alan and Omar's bemusement.

It means terms of business that make sense, are clear, are applied, make rational sense, and are user friendly enough not to occupy primary attention when you're together. You don't want to send across an agreement that requires a legal specialist to unravel.

It means invoices that are readable and have the amount of detail required for processing (client organizations may differ on this, so make sure that this is clarified, otherwise you may find your invoice languishing in an outbox for weeks).

It means that you are willing to be flexible about when you will field certain calls, particularly if you have global clients, and wish to spend more time at home. Omar has found he doesn't mind taking a 10 p.m. call in New York occasionally, if he can do it after a nice meal at home, before a nightcap and a good night's rest in his own bed.

It means you come through on your differentiator. For Leadership Journeys, Omar and his team provide a turnkey service. The client lands at an airport; all the other logistics and aspects of the journey are taken care of, from the rustic aspects to the luxury they end up enveloped in at the finale. The clients get to focus on the experience and the key conversations they are there to have, not whether the bus will show up on time. If you sign up with Alan for a "total immersion" process (see <www.summitconsulting.com>), you spend two days at Alan's home, and you have lunch and dinner together. You get great guidance and superb hospitality. When Omar partook of this as he and Alan were getting to know each other, he was delighted to experience how impeccably Alan comes through on all this.

If you're offering workbooks and CDs, make sure that they are as comprehensive as you've indicated, clear and easy to use, decently packaged, and full of applicable value.

This may seem obvious. But part of global value comes from differentiators that occur and recur *consistently*. This happens when people come to count on them, and when they know they can relax and enjoy that aspect of the experience, instead of worrying about what will be provided each time.

By being easy to do business with, we make ourselves a pleasure to engage. We allow people therefore to focus on receiving the value they have signed up for. Needless to say, ensuring that is the only real demonstration of a consulting partnership that will thrive over time and across any geographical or other boundaries.

Global learning

Great service may linger, but lousy service is immortal in our recollection. Your clients should not be listing you as one of their aggravations, but as someone who helps to make their lives legitimately easier and better.

World tour

- Create value through relationships. Then even your active presence becomes something you can bill for.

- Look for the real needs underlying faddish approaches that are leaving people unfulfilled (for example, customer relationship management, Six Sigma, or building virtual teams).

- Convert different aspects of your expertise into marketable value, and then package it in a way that you can distinctively convey.

- Impact matters, but you have to hang in there enough to also create momentum.

- Pick ways of delivering value that maximize your returns and minimize wear and tear.

- Be a pleasure to do business with.

Travelog

*Great, not so great, odd, and bewildering
aspects of life on the road*

I. Omar

I was asked to speak at a conference hosted by a prominent
sheikh in Abu Dhabi, the capital of the United Arab Emirates.

This was a global conference primarily for young leaders: College
students from around the world would be attending. The headliner
was creativity innovator Edward de Bono, and I
had been recommended as the finale.

A fee of US$15,000 was agreed. I happened
to be in Dubai, so they were taking "pot luck."

With some difficulty, I extended the stay,
drove out from Dubai to Abu Dhabi at 5 a.m. to
make the opening of the conference, waited as
the sheikh arrived 40 minutes late, only to deliver
a ponderous opening that had everyone dozing
off. Finally, Edward de Bono went on. De Bono
took his allotted 60 minutes and was fantastic.
He was followed by a corporate sponsor, who went twice as long as
he should have and demonstrated "death by PowerPoint."

Global takeaway

People often forget that
conferences aren't an
agenda. While time
matters and you should
keep to yours, impact is
what we're there to
create.

The program was running so late that as I was being introduced in glowing terms, an organizer said, "Can you do your entire talk in 15 minutes?" I looked at him bemused. The official, panic stricken that the sheikh might need a tea break said, "Or even shorter, maybe five minutes?" By this time, my introduction had lasted that long!

I didn't debate, went on, and did 30 minutes. The crowd woke up, the college students became engaged, and Edward de Bono clapped loudly and encouragingly, the official grimaced appropriately throughout, and I missed my chance of having one of my most lucrative five minutes ever!

The Young President's Organization (YPO) can be an interesting client when you're getting started. Its membership comprises individuals who are CEOs by age 40, and run businesses with a net enterprise value of at least US$10 million. They pay poorly, but organize wonderfully educational conferences.

Leslie and I went to present at a YPO "University" in Venice, as much for the cultural stimulus of staying in style in Venice for a week, attending a ball at the Doge's Palace, listening to historians, experiencing artists, drinking in the beauty of the world's first watery theme park, and more.

Two gripes were particularly amusing from this well-heeled crowd of CEOs and their spouses. One was a group complaining that they couldn't find any gym in Venice that had the equipment they were after: specifically a Stairmaster! Anyone who has walked around Venice will find that the entire city is a veritable Stairmaster. These same ladies took the touristy gondolas everywhere!

Global takeaway

It helps to remember where we are and to focus more on what is present, not what is absent.

Second, there were two sessions called "Bellini" and "Carpaccio." Not realizing that these are artists, attendees who went hoping to drink the peach juice and champagne concoction or eat the marinated but otherwise raw Italian beef (both of these, by the way, were invented at the famous Harry's Bar in Venice), were miffed at having their art education furthered instead!

Presenting for a two-day leadership retreat for a client in Bangladesh, we were ensconced in the Pan Pacific Hotel. In

Bangladesh, alcohol can only be sold in hotel bars. However, you can take your own to most restaurants. The night before the session, I was taken to an excellent Indonesian restaurant in Dhaka (Indonesian food is big in Bangladesh for whatever reason), with East Asian clients who took several Scotch bottles and tried to recreate a Tokyo drinking evening.

The next day, a spirited, enthusiastic session took place, despite the partying of the night before. Everyone adjourned for the evening and all seemed well.

At 5:30 the next morning, I got a call. Apparently the local government had changed import taxes and duties overnight, which could effectively wipe out the annual profit of this client I was in town for. Given the magnitude of emergency, they asked for a postponement of the second day.

As it turned out, the soccer (football to the rest of the world) World Cup was that day. We decided the time was ripe to become sporting fans. So we nabbed some new friends in the hotel bar, found out what had happened in the tournament to date, and were ready to cheer Brazil (I had been a fan of the legendary soccer star Pele in his youth) on with abundant beer and eclectic spiced popcorn, alongside animated Bengali sports fans!

Global takeaway

The world is not only stranger than we imagine, but as one pundit opined, it is stranger than we can imagine.

When I established a business presence in Dubai, it was helpful to have a resident's visa so I could go in and out easily. At that time, the most straightforward way to be in business was to have a local Arab partner.

One of my clients who was the CEO of one of the major banks in the United Arab Emirates volunteered. He had his local office make the arrangements.

The local office, for which this was a chore, said to me they were going to show my "salary" (you had to state one for the visa) as 5,000 UAE dirhams (about US$1,333 a month). They said that the visa would be unnecessarily more expensive otherwise, so I agreed. The visa was in Arabic.

I noticed that whenever I went to other Arab countries for work, my immigration processing took a long time, and was accompanied by perplexed looks when I said I was there to consult, or give a speech, or whatever. Whenever I went to get local credit cards, the bank executive looked at the documents, scratched his head, and headed off to find a senior manager. They asked for significant extra documentation and many additional references.

After some years of vexation, delays and sometimes just being denied a visa (to Oman, for example), I finally had the resident's visa translated, and found that I had been listed as a "clerk." What the local office of my partner had neglected to tell me was that while it was cheaper, it would interfere with my ability to conduct the very business we were setting up!

After some grumbling from the local office, which disappeared fast after a volcanic outburst from my client/partner, who couldn't believe this had been done, I *finally* graduated from being a clerk in the Middle East!

Global takeaway

Beware of false economies; always invest in what is needed to do business viably.

As are Alan's, my talks are known for provocative comments, and sometimes a splash of racy humor. Also, given my cultural and ethnic background, I can get away with some risqué comments in various parts of Asia—they are accepted and even valued as a necessary wake-up call delivered from "one of us."

On those rare occasions when I return for sessions to Pakistan, a country that to me is quite foreign (because I grew up in New York), I really let rip. The business crowds there love it. Pakistan has a highly educated management cadre, which really would like enough political stability to get on with building its businesses and lives.

Global takeaway

Don't pigeonhole people, and assume you know what they can handle. Although you should always try to be appropriate and respectful with humor, don't inhibit your personality. People usually know where you're coming from.

During one presentation, a man in religious garb approached me. He introduced himself as the Roman Catholic bishop of Islamabad (the country's capital). Christians make up about 10 percent of the population of Pakistan, a nation of about 150 million people. So their numbers aren't insignificant. Alas, they are a persecuted minority there, so the Church leaders have their work cut out for them. Bishop Lobo asked me to run a leadership retreat in the mountains for diocese leaders from around the country.

Some of my colleagues were concerned that these religious people might take umbrage at the playfulness with the audience and the occasional tongue-in-cheek sarcasm that were trademarks of my sessions. During the retreat, at the end of one particularly provocative but stimulating exchange, a nun came up and said, "I love it! Can you come and do this for our novitiates?" For the next several years, that's exactly what we did, for young nuns, initiates, and more!

The European division of one of the largest food and beverage companies in the world asked me to consult because of a "disconnect" between strategy and execution. They had written a hell of a strategy, they said, but it was floundering in execution. The regional CEO asked me to facilitate a three-day "deep dive" to diagnose the root cause and find a way forward. When this was explained to me, the HR leader and CFO nodded thoughtfully at the evident solemnity and importance of the task.

On the morning of the session, I arrived to find the head of HR castigating one of my associates, who was there to help. When I asked what the issue was, the HR boss said seething, "You're putting people at round tables!"

Wondering what I was missing, I explained that with nine leaders, we wanted the flexibility of moving them into different configurations for various conversations. "I feared as much," said the beet-red head of HR. "You can't do that! The marketing and sales directors can't sit together; *they hate each other*!"

I didn't know whether to laugh or cry on their behalf. I nabbed the regional CEO, who had just come in, and explained to him the source of the evident hullabaloo. The CEO looked sheepish, and started inspecting his shoelaces. I said, "I think we've solved the mystery of why your strategy isn't being implemented. Of your nine-person senior regional leadership team, the sales and marketing directors won't even sit at the same table!" I suggested that we either ask for a bit more maturity than that, or abort what would otherwise be a charade.

Global takeaway

Don't look too far up or too far away for where the problems are. Often, as in Edgar Allen Poe's *Purloined Letter*, the causes are hard to see only because they're right under our nose.

The two were placed at the same table, and having survived that trauma, two days later, after several vital and carefully facilitated exchanges, managed even to thaw their relationship enough to start planning how to become the most profitable food and beverage company in the region.

At the end of a three-year consulting engagement for the Philippines operation of a major global beauty company, I was faced with a new head of HR. Alan and I are unanimous in our feeling that if you wanted to prove a counter-Darwinian proposition like *devolution*, you have to look no farther than most HR departments.

Clients develop a certain rhythm with us over time. This client had become assiduous in paying fees and expenses in time. That was so, until the advent of this "buron" (the result when you mate a bureaucrat and a moron). Suddenly, agreed authorized fee payments and expenses were taking months to process.

I escalated this to his contact, the chairman and economic buyer. He interceded, and it was dealt with. However, en route to this, I had dropped a note to this new HR leader, and asked for his assistance, explaining the agreements in place for all these years. A curt reply was sent back, "We are dealing with your payments. However, some advice. In our culture, senior people don't chase payments. If they do, they seem not credible, or desperate. Such notes and follow-up may undermine your effectiveness in this organization as a consultant and coach, and I wouldn't want that to happen."

Global takeaway

Don't let yourself be preached to by internal bureaucrats who are used to brandishing their misguided authority. Don't buy the premise, and get back to that economic buyer fast.

Other than placing a call to the chairman, I told Herr Buron that having helped this company turn itself around over a three-year period, and having been paid US$150,000 to US$200,000 each year to do so, I was comfortable with the credibility established. I also suggested that anyone who thought credibility was increased by not getting paid on time had serious problems, and I thought far better of both the culture there and the people I had gotten to know in the company. The company CFO, upon being asked to get involved by the chairman, agreed as well, expedited the held-up payments, and has been a fertile source of referrals since.

Before I started ensuring that our Leadership Journeys were fully organized by my team, clients sometimes opted to save money by having their own people deal with the logistics aspects.

Heading to Langkawi, Malaysia, in the midst of beautiful rainforests and fascinating mangrove swamps, a major financial services company was sailing from one point to another as part of their journey. It opted, based on a decision from its own administrative people, to sleep overnight on the sailboats. Only after we had anchored for the night, did anyone test the bathrooms. None worked!

The local logistics company (which hadn't been vetted) said it was calling in a locally anchored "cruise ship." People could sleep on board, get some air-conditioning relief from the oppressive humidity, and certainly use the toilets. Everyone cheered.

An hour later, what pulled up alongside the sailboats resembled no cruise ship anyone had ever seen. Rather, it looked like a ghost ship straight out of *Pirates of the Caribbean*. The one crew member on board looked like a relic from *Night at the Museum*, and his canine friend resembled the Hound of the Baskervilles. The "ghost ship" had no air-conditioning, except for three urinals, and unspeakable splatters of something vile everywhere.

Global takeaway

It's great to get away from doing peripheral, non-value-adding things. But never agree to delegate those things that relate directly back to an integral part of what you're offering.

The HR team and administrative staff literally came apart. "Please, do something to help us recover from this tomorrow!" they said plaintively to me.

They needn't have worried. This particular corporate team knew it had botched the arrangements. Amusing as it would have been to hang a few scapegoats from the rafters, the team realized that it *was* a journey, not a pleasure cruise. So why not treat it as an adventure? The next day, the team arrived in stunning Langkawi proper and dove into the fun of its various experiences and the meat of its business conversations with alacrity.

It was, however, the last time I have ever agreed to run a journey for which my team hasn't approved and overseen all the logistics arrangements!

I was booked to do a keynote for a major software and technology company in California (an archrival of Microsoft's). I was told that the two conference chairs would help me prepare.

They told me I had to cover ten points that they had come up with. I told them I didn't work that way (some of the points were so insignificant and trivial I was convinced an audience of this caliber would pelt me with some raw vegetable if I trotted these out). Instead, I asked what impact they were after and what they wanted to accomplish. They answered, "We need to get our leaders to respond creatively to the tremendous challenges we're facing and hear lessons from notable turnarounds."

I replied, "Okay, that I can do. I'll use the points you've mentioned as much as I can. But you're hiring me because of my expertise. You probably don't want to limit the points I may make en route to producing the impact you want." Since one of their vice presidents was a fan of mine from Hong Kong, the relatively junior conference chairs grumbled a bit but went along.

The talk struck the right note. The celebrity founder of this company jumped up, took the mike from me, and said to the global audience listening in by video uplink: "I want you all to send me your examples by email of what he's just explained as soon as he's done. I'm going to make this a major theme for the balance of our conference; this is vital for us."

He then turned to me, and gave me a big thumbs up, and thanked me enthusiastically.

As the talk concluded, many people stood and cheered. But the conference chairs were frowning! They thanked me, and said that it was certainly largely successful, with the key themes covered, but three of their points hadn't been explicitly made!

I said, "But it seems that the impact you wanted was." They couldn't disagree, but still seemed unhappy.

Later, I got a note from the speaker's bureau that had handled the booking, thanking me for the successful talk. but saying that the conference chairs refused to send a testimonial because there were these three points...

Global takeaway

People are buying your expertise. Be accountable for outcomes, not precise steps you'll take. Imagine saying to a surgeon, "Could you do the surgery based on these ten guidelines I just downloaded from the Web?"

The next week, however, I got a call from the global head of marketing saying he had been flooded with requests for copies of the talk from their offices around the world. They had taped an audio version, and asked if I would let them distribute it to all the global offices. I agreed readily, but joked, "Even with those three points missing?" The global VP of marketing said he looked forward to telling the relatively junior hacks who had been made conference chairs what they could do with their three points.

As it is adjacent to one of our client's offices in Bangkok, Leslie and I were booked into the Sofitel, which is also very close to the airport. In Bangkok, being close by is a serious advantage, because the legendary traffic jams there have led some Bangkok veterans to drive with portable urinals!

As we were being checked in, we were handed a keycard and told our suite was on the Club Floor. To access this floor, the key had to be inserted into the appropriate opening in the elevator. We asked for a second key, a normal request for us, and we presume many couples.

There was a pregnant pause, and we were informed that hotel policy was to issue only one key per room.

I was incredulous. "Surely you mean one key per registered guest?"

"No," said the unflappable hotel executive, "one per room; it's for security."

We were tired from an overnight flight, but this was too asinine to agree to. "Suppose my wife is in the salon, I'm at the pool, or we're at different meetings. Do we have to track each other down before getting into our room? Or if I'm having a cigar in the lounge, and she's in the shower, you want me to call her to come down and hand me the key, because I can't even get up in the elevator without the key to ring the bell!"

Global takeaway

Don't let yourself be browbeaten by rules that inherently make no sense. However, also when assisting clients, help them think through not only the stated content or even intent of their business policies, but how they will actually play out in practice.

"It's for your security," he continued to chime mindlessly.

"No, it's not," I said at a point beyond vexation. "It is not for my security to have to shadow my wife all day, or vice versa. I understand that each registered guest should have one key, so extras aren't floating around. But 'protecting' my wife or me, depending on who is in possession of the key at present, from the other in a room we're occupying together is *not* for our security! It's testimony to a poorly thought-out rule at your end..."

A manager came over, could explain the idiocy no better, and issued a second key to appease us, but only after my wife and I both signed a legal disclaimer! We were taking the dread responsibility of dealing with each other's comings and goings on our own heads.

It was a perfectly lovely hotel otherwise, yet afflicted with a policy that had just been misstated so as to render it incomprehensible. When we finally tracked down the general manager, he virtually gagged on the drink he was having with us upon learning what interpretation of their security policy was being applied!

II. Alan

I used to travel according to the most convenient routing. Consequently, there I was one day in Narita Airport flying from Tokyo to Manila on Air Egypt, of all things.

I was sitting in the gate area with the outgoing crew. When the ancient 707 crawled up to the gate, the incoming crew affectionately embraced the outbound crew, which led me to believe these were emotional people or yet another safe landing for Air Egypt.

Global takeaway

Common sense beats intricate consulting models and costs far less.

It was single-class service and chaos. People stood up on the takeoff, and there were chickens somewhere behind me. However, there were also 20 beautiful dancers from a female dance troupe that had toured Japan. They were engaged in tearing apart the boxes of 21 boomboxes they had purchased.

I was told that they were going to pretend that they were not new, so that they could get them through Philippine customs. Three of the dancers approached me, and asked me whether I would carry the twenty-first boombox, purchased for a friend of theirs. They promised to treat me to dinner in Manila. How could I refuse?

At customs (after a landing that dislodged all the oxygen masks), two huge doors flew open, and a dozen heavily armed soldiers arrested all the dancers and ushered them away. That left me and a customs guy who was eyeing *my* boombox.

"Yours?" he asked, looking at my expensive briefcase and business clothing.

"I love music," I mumbled.

He allowed me through, and I wound up in my suite at the Peninsula Hotel. Four hours later, the three girls called from the lobby to reclaim their boombox and take me to dinner.

At dinner, I asked how they tracked me down, since they didn't know where I'd be staying.

"Well," one blushingly admitted, "there are only four top hotels in Manila, and we called all the doormen to see if a dorky American had checked in with a huge boombox. We got you on the second call."

During the same stay in the Philippines, my local business partner and I had to go to Clark Air Force Base, which was a client. We stayed overnight in the bachelor officers' quarters, but I had kept my suite at the Peninsula, eager to return.

The next day, however, featured a horrendous thunderstorm, which shut down all air travel in the area. I put pressure on an air force contact, he put pressure on a Philippine brigadier who had responsibility for all Manila airspace, and we obtained approval for a Cessna to take off out of Clark with a local pilot who volunteered for the job.

> **Global takeaway**
>
> Just because you can do it doesn't mean you should do it. Use standard prudent judgment from home, then double it.

Just as I was bragging to my colleague at about 3,000 feet that I had influence, a violent clap of thunder rocked the plane, and the sky lit up as if we were inside a lightbulb. It was then that I noticed that the old plane's doors weren't flush with the fuselage, and water began to pour in.

The pilot laughed all the way to Manila, while we hung on for dear life. We arrived like drowned rats, but at least there was no baggage wait!

Arriving in Buenos Aires, my local contact picked me up, but was stopped at an improvised checkpoint, where a soldier stuck a submachine gun through the passenger window and started shouting.

My reaction was to panic and bolt (very stupid), but my basic Spanish let me understand that there had been a bomb threat and the soldier was merely warning my colleague not to take certain exits. He probably forgot he was holding the gun.

I was on a speaking tour of Latin America; cell phone use is ubiquitous there. We were doing a US$1,000 per seat seminar in countries where annual per capita income ranged between US$5,000 and US$12,000, and filling up the 250-seat venues.

Despite the cost and the crowd, everyone still used cell phones during the presentation! I was told to just accept it; there was no way around it.

So, halfway through my talk in Bogota, I arranged for my cell phone to ring, took it out of my pocket, and began chatting to a fictional friend. The crowd (we were using simultaneous translation) took two beats, then roared with approval.

Then they went back to their instant messaging!

I was walking down a main, busy street in Rio de Janeiro with a small package I had purchased, when I noticed two young men get up and follow me, and a signal to two more who got up and approached me.

I immediately realized that they wanted to steal the package—or worse—so I took an abrupt left and marched out into the crawling traffic. Horns blared, drivers leaned out their windows to yell at me. A police officer started screaming.

The youths took off. That was the only time in more than 3.5 million air miles of travel that I've been threatened. I acted instinctively and successfully because I was aware of my environment.

Traveling through the English countryside with a local partner, we were making calls on prospects and clients. I had had it with British food and pubs, and was making a nuisance of myself yearning for some good old American "junk" food.

My colleague finally told me that the next town was a decent size and had the equivalent of a TGI Friday's. I looked forward to it all day, and, sure enough, when we entered in the evening, I could have been in Cincinnati or Duluth. I ordered a cheeseburger with the works and fries ("chips").

Then it occurred to me that they might sabotage it with some kind of English cheese. So I said to the server, "What kind of cheese does that come with?"

"Why, melted," she informed me.

My partner fell on the floor, literally, and the two of us had to restore him to a seated position, still howling like a wolf.

Global takeaway

Be careful what you wish for. You can usually make do with the sufficient and don't need the ideal.

I was doing a program for people from six different countries at the Fujiya Hotel in Hakone, near Mt. Fuji in Japan. It was a rollicking good time, and, all of us being internationalists, quickly got down to bragging rights.

A Swiss participant dared me to eat a complete Japanese breakfast for a small sum of money the next morning. I readily agreed, and several others came along to dine and watch the event.

I had eaten these on many occasions—Bento box, varied fish, and so on—but never in this hotel, and, of course, my Swiss friend knew something I didn't. Near the end of my trencherman display, I was presented with a huge snail, out of which I had to extract the slimy creature, which must have been more than two inches long. You couldn't cut it and could barely chew it.

Global takeaway

You can always bank on the fact that people who have done something somewhere before you know more than you about how to do it!

My colleagues grinned as I gamely tackled it. I managed it, and my darer paid for breakfast, but I wasn't the same for days.

I had finished a consulting assignment in Paris, and my wife and I took off to the west to visit Mt. St. Michel. This is the site of the huge tidal fluctuations, and a monastery somehow carved out of the top of a small mountain with stunning views, but a history studded with prisons and hardship.

Hertz had provided the largest car it had, a huge BMW sedan that zipped through the small roads (there is no equivalent to the vast interstate highway system of the U.S. in France, although it does have some major motorways and toll roads run by private companies) passed everything in front of us, and, inexplicably, insisted on "speaking" to us in German.

Once settled into the magical island, we undertook a tour of the cathedral on top. We traveled on foot up the steep hills, then into the edifice, and up through its multiple levels. I'm recently Catholic, but my wife is a lifelong Catholic, and as she turned a corner ahead of me, after 30 minutes of pure climbing, I heard her say, "Jesus, Mary, and Joseph!"

I rushed around the corner to see what miraculous sight awaited us, but it turned out to be thousands more stairs, seeming to lead right up into heaven itself! In another half an hour, we were finally at the top.

The views were stunning, the trip down far easier, and we talk about Maria's religious exclamation to this day.

Global takeaway

Take an extra day, go an extra kilometer, spend an extra euro. The difference between being there and seeing it in the media is the difference between an old tintype and the rainbow. Don't go global and stay local.

Global takeaway

Perspectives differ based on point of origin. Don't assume that the other person has yours, or that you have his or hers. Test what "large," "long," or "complicated" really means. You may find that you're still operating in another time zone.

I was flying across the U.S. from Boston to San Francisco, and the person in the aisle seat was bending to look out my window. I leaned back to accommodate him.

"Striking," he said.

I looked out expecting the Rockies, or the Grand Canyon, or at least a river, but all I saw were flatlands of some Midwestern state.

"What's striking?" I asked.

He explained that he was a German businessman on his first trip to the U.S., and that by this time in the flight he would have flown over five or six European countries.

"We're still in America," he said, impressed, "and we still have more than two hours to go!"

Arriving in Bangkok from Sydney on a worldwide business trip for one client, we found one of my wife's bags missing at the airport. I reported it to the Thai Qantas agent. It was almost midnight, and a limo and hotel suite were awaiting us.

"Our bag is lost," I informed the agent.

"No, it is not," he politely contradicted me.

"Oh, where is it?" I asked.

"We don't know," he said, and I was speechless for once.

"Then it's lost," I pointed out.

"It is *not* lost," he patiently explained. "We simply don't know where it is yet."

My wife put her hand on my arm, I stopped arguing, and signed the claim form. We left, the limo took us to the Regent Hotel, where the manager informed us he was pleased to upgrade us to the presidential suite.

Two days later, sitting next to our grand piano, a porter brought the missing suitcase, without a word, and departed. It had, extraordinarily, been to Heathrow, through a fire there, returned to Australia, and back to us. It had more frequent flyer miles than I did.

At that moment, the phone rang, and the same Qantas agent called to tell me that they still didn't know where my bag was.

"But it's not lost," I said.

"It's not lost," he patiently reiterated. "We just don't know where it is."

"Oh, but I do!" I told him.

Global takeaway:

Fight for the major issues, values, ethics, and critical elements. Don't sweat the small stuff, especially internationally. You'll wind up just fine, often in a splendid suite with a well-traveled bag and a smile on your face.

Part III

The Journey

Chapter 7

Applying Value-Based Fees

*Your time is not the issue and
had better not be*

Value-based fees comprise a system of establishing fees for consulting services based on the consultant's contribution to the value the client receives as a result of the project objectives being met. Although the phrase (as well as "value-based pricing") has become popularized in many forms, the concept was pioneered and formalized for the solo practitioner in the late 1980s by Alan Weiss, and popularized in his landmark books on the subject.[1]

In essence, basing fees on value rather than time units, numbers or people, labor, or materials is the most ethical and lucrative way to receive compensation from clients. *It is important to domestic consultants who wish to acquire wealth, and absolutely mandatory for those attempting to generate seven figures across borders,* because time units are very expensive for the consultant internationally.

The philosophy of value-based fees

Value-based fees are based on this underlying belief: The consultant's compensation is based on his or her contribution to significant business outcomes, which provide a dramatic return on investment for the client and equitable compensation for the consultant.

This isn't a bad phrase to learn, because it's the ideal response for a buyer who inquires about your fee basis, since the buyer is probably incorrectly educated by past consultants who charge by the time unit. Take a minute to consider it, mark this page, and later on, *when you're convinced*, memorize so that you can say it conversationally.

Value-based fees are not retainers (although retainers can and should be value based), performance fees, or deposits. They might be called "project fees," although we're not crazy about that phrase, either. They are set based on the consultant's contribution to value. (Whereas a lawyer's "retainer" is really a deposit against future hourly billing, and a lawyer's "contingency fee" is a piece of the action; both practices we find ethically obnoxious.)

As you can see in Figure 7.1, value traditionally follows fee. That is, the more you value something, the more you will pay for it. These decisions are often emotional. No one needs a Mercedes-Benz for transportation or a Bulgari watch to tell the time. But the status and cachet of owning (and displaying) them are key motivators. As a rule, logic makes people think, but emotion makes them act. (You can take that to the bank in your consulting work when you're trying to achieve organizational change, as well.)

However, what Alan discovered when he began his practice in 1985, the lines cross! There is a point at which value begins to follow fee, meaning that people expect to get what they pay for.

No one expects that the watch is a Rolex if they've paid a guy on the corner US$29, or the pen a Cartier if the seller asks for US$12. Sometimes the simple act of paying a great deal of money provides the proof of the value.

But the dynamic isn't merely psychological. That point at which the lines cross represents powerful branding. It's one thing to say, "Get me a terrific strategy consultant" and the name of Jane Jones is in that group. But it's far better to say, "Get me Jane Jones!"[2] When you are the "go to" person, *the* expert, the referral from a respected source, then you are worth whatever the fee may be.

Global learning

Value-based fees will ultimately safeguard the client as well as pay you what you deserve. They are win-win.

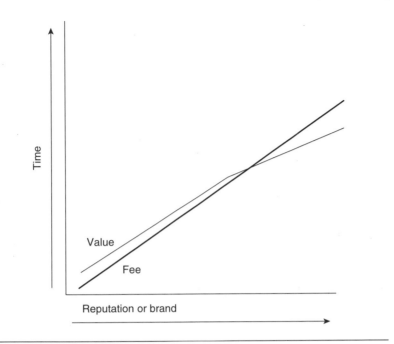

Figure 7.1   Value follows fee

Another consideration for understanding value-based fees is that they protect the client. That may seem counterintuitive, but consider this: The client, ethically, is best served through the quickest resolution of the client's issue. If the consultant makes less money through quick resolution and more money through slow resolution, that is a client-unfriendly system.

Alan interviewed bookkeepers when he moved to Rhode Island. One of the interviewees revealed that she refused to use a computer, believing that hand posting was far better. "Isn't it much slower?" inquired Alan innocently.

"Yes," she admitted, "but I'm very careful and take all the time I need."

"How do you charge?" he asked.

"Why, by the hour, of course!"

So Alan was being asked to pay extra for this person's refusal to use time-saving devices and her deliberately slow pace. He was to subsidize her snail-like work pace.

At least that was transparent and innocent. Omar had a client, Jesper, who was heading up a Maersk operation in South Asia. His office set him up with several realtors to select a home to rent for him and his family.

One realtor had a distinctive approach. He interviewed Jesper, found out his desires and needs and those of his family, and came back with a video CD that provided a virtual tour of houses he thought would fit the bill. Jesper and his family viewed them, and short-listed them to three they would see in person. Then in one morning they went out, made their choice, and signed the papers.

This realtor charged a fair bit more, so Jesper's office colleagues were scandalized. "He only took you out for two hours, and spent maybe an afternoon creating that video CD! Other realtors spent days with you, and he gets more for a few hours!"

Jesper chuckled and said to his colleagues, "So you want me to penalize him for being smarter, saving me time, saving himself time, and delivering the value I wanted in an innovative way? You recommend that instead, I reward inefficiency and lack of imagination?" Indeed not.

So when we only make money by staying longer, protracting projects, and (anathema for global consulting) logging on-site time, we are cheating the client or cheating ourselves, or both. That's simply not a world either of us choose to live in when it is so easily avoided.

We've both completed many major projects where we never had to show up, or were on site for the barest minimum of time at the outset and end. Modern technology simply reinforces the ease with which we can consult for and support our worldwide clients.

But the enabler is knowing that we don't have to be present (or even logging the lawyerly 15-minute increments off site) to be paid well.

What follows is a quick course in value-based fees. You can read any number of Alan's books on the subject if you need more detail.

Just remember that the reason more consultants aren't using value-based fees is not client resistance. It's consultant recalcitrance.

The fundamentals of value-based pricing

Value-based fees require clear business outcomes upon which the client can place a value. *The value needn't always be quantitative, such as a two percent increase in sales.* Qualitative objectives, such as increased reputation, lowered stress, and greater comfort are all fine business outcomes, depending on the client.

Here are the three keys to establishing value-based fees:

1. Establish objectives

Objectives are business results. "A clearer understanding of strategy" is not a business result, merely an improved skill. But "Creating unified decision making across departments in consistent support of our strategy" is a dramatic business outcome. The consultant's efforts are usually the same, but the description of the actual output makes all the difference.

Similarly, "Facilitate 12 focus groups" is merely part of the delivery methodology, not worth very much, and merely a commodity. But "Create employee inclusion so that the new compensation plan is quickly accepted and cost savings realized" is quite a dramatic outcome.

Look at your past several proposals. Are you quoting inputs and methodology, or outputs and business results? This is a simple *but absolutely vital element* in creating value-based fees.

Note that objectives must come from the buyer: The question is: "What will look, feel, or sound better once this project is completed?"

2. Establish measures of success

Next, you need metrics. To use Bob Mager's famous phrase about training objectives, "How would you know if you fell over it?" What measures will the buyer use to determine the progress being made toward the objectives and when they are realized?

Some metrics are quantitative: Numbers of new sales, shortened duration of meetings, greater retention of new hires, and fewer customer complaints are all examples. But some are anecdotal: Serving less as a referee among competing teams, feeling more comfortable in front of the media, hearing improved comments about the company's image, and more relaxing and productive retreat settings are examples of relying on the buyer's senses.

Note that metrics must come from the buyer. The question is: "How will you know that the goals are being met?"

3. Establish the value of the project

Now we're ready to understand the basis for our fees. We want to know the worth, impact, and value to the organization and the buyer of meeting the objectives. That is, there must be a salutary business improvement from the objectives being met.

Sometimes, the value seems intrinsic and obvious: If the objective is a 12 percent increase in profit, then what more is there to ask? But always go a step further. What is the impact of a 12 percent increase in profits? The buyer, if guided, will probably include issues such as increase in shareholder value; more funds to support future R&D efforts; ability to buy back stock or pay off indebtedness; or attracting a more favorable rating for the management team from Wall Street.

Most consultants never arrive at agreement on value, so don't be dissuaded. The value may be organizational or personal, or both. Push this issue.

Note that value must come from the buyer. The question is: "What will the impact of meeting those objectives as determined by those metrics be for the organization and for you?"

Objectives, measures, and value must be established with the buyer, the person who can authorize payment for the project without any other approvals or involvement. We call this person the "economic buyer" (as opposed to mere "feasibility buyers"[3]). "Conceptual agreement" occurs when you review these three critical elements with your buyer and the buyer agrees, without qualification, that they are valid for the project. *Note that this comes before any proposal ever being written.*

Global learning

All bets are off if you're not talking to a true buyer—an "economic buyer." That is the person who can authorize your payment. The economic buyer is never a committee.

If you follow this advice, you may submit fewer proposals, but you should see 80 percent of them accepted. That's the ratio for us and for people in Alan's Global Mentor Program of more than 13 years' duration.

Base your fee on a dramatic return on investment (ROI). In other words, if the total of the quantitative and qualitative value is US$750,000, then a US$75,000 fee provides a 10:1 return, which is far more than most organizations derive in any activity other than money laundering! If the project worth is US$6 million, and you perceived your role in that result to be about one-third, that would result in a US$200,000 fee (a tenth of US$2 million). Of course, you can use 5:1 or 20:1, depending on your style, relationships with the client, expertise, scarcity, and so on.

Vignette

Alan was working with the CEO of a US$600 million animal health company. All of the CEO's objectives were qualitative.

Paul wanted to stop playing referee among competing teams and interest groups; to improve the environment of his executive floor; and to provide an image to the board of being in control and on top of all breaking events.

Alan knew that Paul was making US$1.5 million, including a modest bonus in an average year. He also knew that Paul's personal goals were to be considered a "star" in the parent company and to move up to corporate leadership from amid a very competitive group of subsidiaries.

The project was accepted at US$135,000. Both Paul and Alan felt that it was a great deal. Could it have been US$110,000 or US$160,000? Perhaps. But so what? It's all profit, it's a great piece of business, the client was delighted, and life went on.

Fee setting is art and science. Don't overlook the art.

One of our favorite techniques is to get the client to agree on the value *and then cut it in half to be extraordinarily conservative.* Now the client is receiving a 10:1 return on half of his or her own estimate, making it far greater according to his or her original estimate.

$$\frac{\text{Tangible Outcomes} \times \text{Expected Duration} + }{\text{Intangible Outcomes} \times \text{Emotional Impact} + } \\ \frac{\text{Peripheral Benefits} \times \text{Variables Positively Affected}}{\text{Fixed Investment}} = \frac{\text{CLIENT}}{\text{VALUE}}$$

Figure 7.2 A fee formula

In case you need it, we've provided a formula for helping to visualize your value in Figure 7.2.

Overcoming objections and creating converts

The main objections to value-based fees come from clients who have been overwhelmingly miseducated by other consultants. Here are the key techniques to counter these objections.

Global learning

If you are discussing fees and not value, you've lost control of the discussion.

- Never cite a daily rate, materials cost, or per-person charge. If a buyer asks, "What are your rates?," simply reply, "I don't have rates. I charge a single, agreed fee once we establish your needs and the scope of the project." Never allow yourself to be persuaded to talk about fees in advance of conceptual agreement on objectives, measures, and value.
- Emphasize the buyer's self-interest. Here's a great line: "There is never a meter running with me. I would never put you in a position where you had to make an investment decision every time you or your people thought you might need me or my advice."
- Demonstrate the ethical underpinning. "It's an inherent ethical conflict for me to make money the longer I'm here when you are best served by a rapid and high-quality resolution."
- Discuss the non-consulting background of larger consulting firms. Most come from the audit business originally, in which hourly billing is critical to keep human assets profitable. They are production capability driven. You, on the other hand, are driven by the results of the services you provide.
- Always provide options in your proposal. If you provide a single alternative, the buyer has a "take it or leave it" choice. But if you

provide three or four options, the buyer has a range of choices. It's the difference, psychologically and powerfully, between "Should I use Alistair" and "*How* should I use Alistair?" That's a profoundly different choice.

- Focus on the ROI. Remind the buyer that he or she developed the value estimates, and that you then took only a smaller percentage of them to be conservative, and even those represent a 10:1 (or better) return on the investment. Ask the buyer where else that kind of return is being realized.

- Cite the fact that no two clients are ever the same and that you don't use off-the-shelf or "cookie-cutter" approaches. Stress that you are a consultant who focuses on ends, not means, and that you design the means only to best suit the particular client's ends.

- Never allow yourself to be delegated to lower-level people. Human resources people and trainers *are paid to conserve budget*. But economic buyers *are paid to achieve results*. If they find significant value, they'll make an ROI calculation and find the money they need to invest. HR people will *never* do that, because they don't have the power, and it's far too threatening. Tell the buyer that these are strategic decisions, and can only be made by him or her.

- Demonstrate that your fee system actually protects the project. Whereas an ongoing billing of hourly or daily charges can be peremptorily halted at any time, value-based fees cannot be so readily stopped, because the investment has often already been made.[iv]

- Do not become part of an RFP (request for proposal) process. These invariably are evaluated by low-level people who put an emphasis on cost savings, not results, and are systems in which you rarely will get to meet the buyer to forge conceptual agreement. (We'll talk about how to circumvent these entirely in the section that follows.)

The absolutely critical competitive advantage in using value-based fees is that they help you avoid—perhaps absolutely avoid—becoming a commodity. Many clients, and virtually all human resources departments, ordinarily treat consultants as merely another species of vendor. They see us as no different, from a purchasing standpoint, from the people who pave the parking lot, or sell computers, or service the vehicles.

Once you are seen as a commodity, and present hourly fees, or workshop prices, or numbers of days, you will be compared with others who are perceived as providing the same kind of *deliverables*. The notion of "deliverables" is anathema to consultants.

We are not vendors. Our value is not in "deliverables" (which should be minimized in any case to decrease labor intensity). We should not be readily comparable with the people down the street.

So the education of the true, economic buyer is essential if we are to avoid being seen as readily duplicatable sources that can be compared solely on the basis of price.

Omar was asked by a global client to provide some coaching support for one of their vice presidents in charge of corporate acquisitions. This VP was clearly skilled and competent, but various recent experiences had rattled his confidence. Emotionally, he was flailing around, unsure of his standing and how to make the biggest impact in this role.

In assessing this, Omar was able to elicit that in this industry, scale was everything, and so to grow, the client had to acquire smaller companies and offer a consolidated service to their customers. So the VP of acquisitions was a critical role.

This company was currently a US$500 million turnover operation, producing about US$150 million in profit. The CEO estimated that if the company successfully landed two key acquisitions, led by this VP, it would add about US$300 million to its turnover and about 30 percent to its profitability. This strategic undertaking wouldn't just be thanks to this one VP of course, but he would be a major influence in it.

Omar was passing through London anyway several times in the coming months, and the CEO agreed to have the VP intersect with Omar there during those landings.

Having established all this, the CEO had no sticker shock at all when Omar quoted US$35,000 for the quarter. Omar declined to commit to how many face-to-face meetings would occur. He indicated they could have more meetings if needed, less too if a breakthrough occurred.

The HR person almost passed out. "You're charging US$35,000 for up to three one-hour coaching meetings and a few calls and email?" Omar replied, "No, for helping to ensure your vice president successfully helps you make the acquisitions necessary to grow your business strategically. It's a bargain at twice the price."

Only two face-to-face coaching sessions were needed in that quarter. Several acquisitions later, Omar has an avid fan and an ongoing client, and no one has ever scrutinized the invoices since.

In our experience, almost all of the failures to implement value-based fees successfully originate with the consultant, not the buyer. That's because there is a failure of preparation, persuasion, or will.

The first value-based fee sale is to yourself. Stand in front of the mirror and say, calmly, "The fee is ninety thousand dollars." Don't giggle, don't gag, don't grab the furniture for support.

If you can't convince that buyer, you can't convince anyone.

Using-value based pricing internationally

There are even greater reasons to use value-based fees across borders. As we've developed our international practices, we've thanked the fates that we had this vital tool in our bag from the beginning. We want you to have that same advantage, so that you can build wealth immediately.

You must reduce labor intensity

This book is about using modern technology, brand, and referral business to operate globally *without having to visit every single place every single day,* which is clearly neither possible nor desirable. Even if you've managed a fairly labor-intensive practice domestically, equaling that internationally will kill you. That amount of travel will strain your endurance, your spirit, and your relationships. If you have family, which most of you do, this is an even more critical factor.

Look at it this way: Spending a day locally is just that. Spending a day, say, a thousand miles away in your own country or a country nearby is probably close to three days, including travel and allowing sufficient contingent time. But spending a day a ten-hour or more plane ride away requires almost five days, allowing for acclimatization and the same contingencies. That means that if you don't change your labor intensity, *you're going to be four or five times more exhausted, missed, behind on the mail, and away from the dogs!*

A brief digression: If you're thinking that you can overcome this by combining trips and taking two weeks to visit three clients and then return, *fuggedaboudit!* Long international trips that change time zones are exhausting, even with first-class travel and accommodations, and they place you even further behind your routine and loved ones.

The only way to make significant money if you're reducing your labor intensity with international travel is by using value-based fees, so that your presence doesn't generate your income.

You must overcome rigid procurement policies and RFPs

As stated, many international firms use RFPs as their basis for hiring consultants. They are antagonistic to anything but time-based fees.

The way around this is to become a "sole source" provider. That means that you, alone, are right for the particular project, and competitive bidding would be of no help. (This is also useful for government purchasing, by the way, especially in the U.S.) You can become a sole source provider in any number of ways, including:

- being a book author on a relevant topic. Only you have written that particular book
- having intellectual property that is unique and required for the project
- experiences that make you uniquely qualified to handle the project (international clients, military background, industry familiarity, and so on)
- educational credentials: Ph.D. in organizational psychology, MBA, professional engineer, and so forth.

The ability to use retainers

Retainers are access to your smarts. We'll say that another way: Retainers are access to your smarts. Okay, now you say it.

This is not the typical attorney retainer, which we've pointed out is merely hourly billing in disguise. It is a payment to you to be available. It is not project work.

Many high-level clients want you to be their sounding board, coach, and confidant. The issue here is accessibility, not proximity. If you can guarantee reasonable response time, or agree on some nonstandard telephone hours, then you can serve this purpose from anywhere in the world.

Retainer fees are based on three main criteria:

- How many people have access? Is it just the client, or also the four direct reports of the client? Normally, you need to limit this number severely, but you should also place a premium on a group, rather than a single person.

Global learning

A retainer may be the most powerful value-based fee technique that can be used across borders because access needn't be in person.

- What is the scope of the access? Is it during the client's business week, your business week, weekends? Can the client expect phone calls returned within, say, six hours? Can the client set up phone calls that, for you, come at midnight (or worse)? Can the client expect email response within, say, six hours?
- What is the duration? As a rule, don't accept retainers for less than 90-day periods. Always collect the fee at the *beginning* of the period.

Depending on these three variables, establish a retainer fee, for example, US$10,000 per month or US$30,000 for the coming quarter, and you're ready to roll. Except you're not rolling. You're staying at home, a vital resource to a key executive somewhere on the globe connected to you at almost any time.

Your ability to function internationally, much more your potential to make seven figures across borders, will absolutely depend on your ability to use value-based fees competently and confidently. Make no mistake about it, if you work internationally and charge for time units or deliverables, you'll soon wish you never obtained a passport.

World tour

- You must educate (or re-educate) the buyer to use value-based fees.
- You must deal with an "economic buyer," someone who can authorize a check for you without further approvals.
- You must have conceptual agreement about objectives, measures of success, and value to the organization before establishing fees.
- You can overcome the inherent problems of RFPs and dealing with the human resources department if you follow this philosophy.
- Retainer business is the ultimate form of value-based fees, and constitutes a superb cross-border strategy.

Endnotes

1. For example, see *Million Dollar Consulting* (McGraw-Hill, 1992, 1998, 2002) and *Value Based Fees* (Jossey-Bass/Pfeiffer, 2nd Edition, 2008), among others.
2. The ultimate brand is always your name. More about that in chapter 9.
3. People in human resources or the training department are virtually never economic buyers, and should never be courted or given proposals, especially when you're engaged in global business.
4. Because you should normally seek payment terms of 50 percent at the outset and 50 percent in 45 days, or provide a 10 percent reduction for full fee paid at the outset. See Alan's books for instructions on how to present such payment plans.

Chapter 8

Adding Value Across Cultural Distinctions

What you shouldn't adapt is as important as what you should

It is a reliable badge of faith that cultural adaptation and nimbleness are important advantages to global consulting success. Essentially, this is correct. There is no justification for antagonizing clients or colleagues with our cultural illiteracy, and certainly the applicability of our counsel has to factor in both the realities and at times some of the cadences and rhythms of life in the environments in which we find ourselves.

Moreover, anybody who has consulted or coached for some time knows that one of the barriers to change is defensiveness. Confronted with our own culpability, many try to attack the advice, or else claim it is inapplicable to us, or if all else fails, then to blame external fate or feckless colleagues or employees. When that happens, generally, it is necessary to be able to stand one's ground intellectually and emotionally. This is also needed in the face of cultural diversionary tactics or smokescreens, if attempted.

All of that said, much of what determines consulting effectiveness applies across borders.

What makes a good leader, for example, is fairly universal. Attributes include the ability to craft visionary objectives, strategic clarity, taking effective judgment calls, executing plans and following through, being an accomplished talent scout and success coach, having solid market intuition, being able to challenge flaccid thinking, applicable market intuition, being able to build and guide teams where needed, being meritocratic, and practicing what Stanford professor and IDEO alumnus Bob Sutton calls *Vu ja De* (as opposed to *"deja vu,"* which is a feeling that something unknown to us is strangely familiar or has been experienced before, *"vu ja de"* is seeing something that we know and *is* familiar in a different and therefore potentially transformational way).

These leadership variables are remarkably consistent around the world. They may be expressed slightly differently in different cultures, with more or less charisma or more or less directness, but you'll be able to spot a leader just about anywhere on this basis.

We have found unequivocally that we are more similar than dissimilar as humans and as businesspeople around the block or around the world.

Moreover, when people decide to partner with you and have you as their advisor and ally, they will be more interested in your originality, authenticity, and imagination than whether you can morph yourself into a cultural lookalike. They are looking for a partner who can help them raise their game, not a chameleon.

Experience it yourself

Well before the media discovered Dubai, the American head of FMC there asked Omar for a favor. "I know it's not what you do," said Bill, "but I need some help acclimatizing some key executives who are very nervous about moving here." Omar asked why exactly they were nervous. Bill, now a fervent fan of life in Dubai, said, "CNN, paranoia, misinformation, take your pick."

It transpired that these four executives and their spouses had been sent in the U.S. to a cultural orientation class in which the Middle East was spoken of as one large undifferentiated cultural mass. Most of the warnings related to Saudi Arabia. They were told that women couldn't drive, that very modest dress was called for, to never mention their religion, or discuss politics, that you certainly couldn't drink in public or eat pork, and so on.

Well, these are all true in Saudi Arabia because the ruling House of Saud struck a deal when these countries were being carved out with the extremist Wahhabi sect as a way to keep the Hashemites at bay (a far more temperate clan and rulers of modern-day Jordan) and extend their own regional influence. Dubai, in particular, is a liberal oasis by comparison. It is the Las Vegas of the Middle East.

These executives and their spouses were shocked to find pork sold in supermarkets, ladies wearing miniskirts and bikinis that were gaze-diverting to say the least, women executives, Eric Clapton concerts, Tiger Woods playing golf in the Desert Classic, Bill Clinton and Rudy Giuliani discussing politics animatedly at conferences, and pubs and wine bars overflowing with good cheer. They were mystified, and concerned. They kept waiting for the other shoe to fall.

Omar spent a few days with them, introducing them around, explaining some of the cultural realities underneath the modern gloss, sharing some sensitivities to be aware of, but essentially confirming that they were in a modern city that was proud of the visionary choice their rulers had made when confronted with a relative shortage of oil compared with their neighbors.

So don't believe everything you read or are told. Ensure that the sources are solid, and be suspicious of generalizations. It is important to know where you are, as a consultant and as a traveler. But then keep your own eyes open, and develop a base of experience that will allow you your own "take" on the place. As these FMC employees found, that was far more productive than the drivel shared with them at the bizarre States-side course they had attended.

Global learning

Consultants are expected to test assumptions and check facts. Don't lose this aptitude or attitude when visiting new countries or experiencing diverse cultures.

In the "for better or for worse" department, Americans are often the worst at making cultural adaptation and *not* making cultural adaptation. Alan has spent too many days sitting in beautiful hotel lobbies with professionally attired local colleagues and clients watching American tourists in T-shirts and flip-flops, as identifiable as giant pandas.

Be attuned to where and with whom you are interacting

In consulting and speaking settings, this applies very powerfully. Omar was addressing the annual conference of Singapore Airlines.

He was speaking of leadership in action, as opposed to just leadership in theory. The talk was going well, with healthy exchanges and a high degree of audience engagement.

As Omar made the point that we need creative contention often to crack the carapace of some of our cherished but unsupportable assumptions, a senior leader stood up shaking his head. "Mr. Khan, I've enjoyed your talk up until now, and we've learned a lot. But I can't go along with this point. You Westerners are infatuated with this Hegelian dialectic (no kidding, these were his precise words) of thesis, antithesis, synthesis. We in the East don't believe such fighting is productive; we believe in harmony."

This could have thrown a major monkey wrench into the talk and the proceedings. This is why it is so important to have some idea of not only the culture, but some of the likely philosophical outlooks at play there.

Omar thanked the leader for the input, and then pointed out that creative contention is used also in Zen Buddhism, where lessons are often presented in contradictory and paradoxical forms, and resolving these is meant to be a way to wisdom. Many of the martial arts (for example *aikido*, which Omar had studied for years) are based on redirecting force, the very essence of creative contention.

One way to protect a potentially challenging insight while offering an alternative and enlarged view is a technique called a "reframe." You put an alternative perceptual frame around what has happened so that everyone can see it in a different, healthier context.

Omar pointed out that the leader raising his point had actually reduced harmony in the room... temporarily! But had he held back, disagreed but kept smiling, that would have been *hypocrisy*, not harmony. Now that they were engaging, they had a chance to learn from each other, to revise each other's views, or to agree to respect differences. Real dialogue, and potentially real harmony, was now possible.

Many people nodded, and Omar even got a smile and a wink from this senior leader. The talk carried on to a successful conclusion. Thankfully, Omar, knowing something about the ideologies and perspectives of the region, was able to "reframe" the concern. However, he didn't change his talk to stay politically correct. It would have been disingenuous, and no one would have learned anything or gotten much value. However, had he been flummoxed by the point of view, he would have done a disservice to either the audience or the point he was seeking to make.

Sometimes, not understanding each other's communication styles can stymie attempts to connect and to collaborate.

Another East Asian client, Mary, asked Omar to help her with the following quandary. Her U.K.-based American boss, Ray, and her predominantly European team complained that she wasn't expressive enough and seemed uncommunicative. Yet they all said that when she spoke, it was always worth listening to. She was quite distraught, asking Omar why these colleagues of hers felt the need to speak at such length, beat around the bush, and take so long to come to the point or commit to action.

Omar then had a chance to offer some perspective, both to her as an East Asian and to her boss, an American living and working in London.

To Mary, Omar pointed out that people schooled and brought up in the West often speak as a mode of thinking. We talk things out, we shoot the breeze, and we try ideas out. She might have to not think of discourse and the sharing of ideas and feelings, if not precisely tailored to action, to be a waste. It was a mode of relating, and a working through of options.

Mary was genuinely surprised, as though she hadn't considered this. "Do you really mean this?" she asked. Omar assured her he did.

To Ray, Omar had to explain that those schooled in East Asia are taught to process their thoughts privately. They speak either as a form of social punctuation, or to relay information, or to convey a conclusion that can precipitate action. So to elicit more dialogue and exchange from Mary, Ray would have to allow her more space, more time, and he'd have to be less uncomfortable with a pause for her to gather her thoughts.

Global learning

The world as we mentally process it seems utterly natural to us. The problem is, this also applies to everyone else and the way they mentally process the world! There's no quicker way to get derailed as we travel in the world than to lose sight of this.

These may seem like obvious bits of guidance. But her American boss and her European team, who valued Mary's inputs and wanted more of them, occasionally had to create an opening for her. Mary, in turn, learned not to get agitated if the conversation occasionally meandered, and knew that people wanted to know what she was thinking and feeling, not just her final conclusion.

When you understand differences in educational approach, processing styles, tempo, and beliefs about how and when to contribute, you can provide great value in helping clients whose teams are made up of different nationalities and reflexes, to build bridges, rather than fortify barriers.

Celebrating together

One of the best ways to establish rapport, to build and strengthen relationships, and often to get fascinating cultural insight, is to understand the nature of celebrations in various cultures and locales.

A client, a peripatetic Frenchman now based in Morocco, tracked Omar down one December 23 in Hong Kong. Omar and Leslie were in Hong Kong for Christmas. Unlike Western observances of Christmas, which are about family togetherness and perhaps church services, in Hong Kong, Christmas celebrations include fireworks, New Year-type countdowns, and people thronging the streets at midnight. It's quite a scene!

Returning from dinner, Omar was surprised to find a message from this client to please call him. Omar did, and found that Laurent, head of marketing in Morocco for a global financial services company, wanted a quick input from Omar relative to a career-critical presentation on January 5. He was calling now because he was going to be incommunicado himself from December 24 until January 4. They spent about 15 minutes on the phone, and Laurent apologized profusely for bothering Omar. Knowing how seriously Laurent and his family take Christmas as observant Catholics in France, Omar told him not to worry; he knew how important it was.

Relaxing somewhat, Laurent then asked Omar what time it was in Hong Kong. "It's 10:30 in the evening," said Omar. The naturally jocular Frenchman relocated his *joie de vivre*: "Ah, then you are only back in your room for a brief break, a respite, *n'est-ce pas* [translated: "isn't that so?"]? The night is young, you are about to head out for another bottle of champagne I'm sure, for some dancing..."

Knowing Omar and Leslie were in Hong Kong for a getaway, Laurent felt okay in leaving a message for Omar to call if he could. Knowing Laurent and the importance of Christmas to him, for Omar, it was a call he was willing to make for this person at this time, who he knew certainly wouldn't be calling casually. This cultural calibration and awareness can help you take those key judgment calls and thereby fortify your relationships.

Global learning

Develop a database of insights and observations about places, cultures, and even specific clients that can help you peg the best approaches, responses and initiatives—including the best occasions for them.

On the other hand, if you have ever been in France, for example, over or near the weekend of Pentecost, you know how seriously it is taken and how complete the shutdown is for that long weekend. Wise consultants will avoid that week and perhaps the frantic few days after, just as they will avoid the week of and the week after Chinese New Year, which is virtually a total shutdown across East Asia for any marketing visits or follow-up plans.

This awareness can also help in marketing and winning new business despite apparent "no go" times. For example, although Ramadan (the Muslim month of fasting based on a lunar calendar) is a time throughout the Muslim world (the Middle East, East Asian countries such as Indonesia and Malaysia, parts of South Asia, Morocco) when delivering work is largely out (people don't concentrate very well on business improvement when they're abstaining from food and water from sun-up to sundown), it's a great month for marketing. Because people are supposed to be at work during this month, not on holiday, executives throughout these regions can be found at home, available for appointments, and very willing to *book* work for other periods of the year. Because most global consultants give these countries a wide berth over this period, there's very little competition for time and attention!

Finally, some holidays and celebrations have more whimsy than solemnity to them. But again, understanding them gives you wonderful insight into the host culture. All of this is grist for your communication and interaction mill.

In England, Guy Fawkes Day, November 5, is still celebrated with fireworks (somewhat constrained these days because of security concerns) and bonfires, with effigies being burned of the conspirator Guy Fawkes, who planned to blow up Parliament and King James I on the day the monarch was to open Parliament in 1605. It's a testament to the droll humor of the British that so narrow an escape for the king and Parliament (thanks to a tip received in the nick of time) has been converted into so enduring an occasion of hearty, insouciant good cheer. To us, this provides endearing insight into the way many Brits process the world.

Reasons to ignore cultural variance

Now let's earn our stripes as contrarians. If we look at leaders who have made a major impact on their businesses and perhaps their societies, we think of people such as Jack Welch, Akio Morita (of Sony), Carlos Ghosn (who engineered Nissan's turnaround in Japan), W. Edwards Deming (the American who founded TQM in Japan after being resolutely ignored at home), Nelson Mandela, Lee Kuan Yew (the architect of modern-day Singapore). Did they make a global impact by adapting their communication to multiple audiences or mellowing the power of their primary passion? No, rather their message and example transcended both the limits of the cultures from which they originated and the boundaries of the cultures many of their listeners came from.

People are led more by those who jolt them awake than by those who placate and pander to them. We doubt any of the named leaders was ignorant about the many varieties of peoples and cultures he was engaging with. But each realized that leadership is first about authenticity, about finding your original voice. It is only secondarily about adapting that to make inroads with others. If the content is valuable enough, if the commitment to add value is truly genuine, people will stretch themselves to understand you, and gain even more from that than when you mutate your message to their cultural "default setting".

Global learning

Learn to sift out the hokum and "static" surrounding cultural sensitivity as opposed to real cultural empathy and rapport. With clients, we have to help expand paradigms, not just capitulate to them.

Many of the famous tomes about cultural sensitivity highlight the many different habits and preferences that exist around the world. We are warned that many oriental cultures consider it rude if you don't slurp your noodles and if you don't emit a contented belch at the end of the meal. We are warned that shaking hands with your left hand in many cultures is considered unclean. That it would be as rude to thump a Japanese on the back as it would be silly to be offended when receiving that treatment from an Italian or a Greek.

These are doubtless good things to know, so we don't misunderstand the reactions or civility of others. But they are not good as an inducement to begin to ape each and every one of these things ourselves! Does anyone seriously believe that you will be ultimately judged as a consultant or business colleague on whether you belch, or which hand you break the camel meat off with in a traditional Bedouin dinner (right hand please)? People may be charmed when you know about their mores, when your tonsils aren't cowardly in slamming back an iced vodka in Moscow, or discovering you appreciate truffles from Alba, or that you enjoy your ballet as well as *bunraku* (puppet theater in Japan), and that you know how to "win friends and influence people" in Sri Lanka or Pakistan by enthusiastically sharing your knowledge of cricket. But honestly, who *really* judges you *primarily* for anything substantial on this basis?

Perhaps if two business rivals are absolutely indistinguishable, such "icing" will determine the outcome. But otherwise, don't kid yourself. Getting to know your client or partner, understanding the market, offering powerful and distinctive value, being willing to be educated on what matters culturally to that specific person or group (rather than necessarily arriving as a generic "expert"), that's how you get ahead locally *or* globally.

This gets us to the problem underlying giving an exaggerated importance to this variety of cultural sensitivity. We can accept that the descriptions of what various cultures are like are usually statistically truer than not. But they often blind you to looking at people with open minds, eyes, hearts, and so on. Are all Americans outspoken and bombastic? Are all Japanese shy and retiring? Are all French people cultured and standoffish? Are all Indians enterprising, but paradoxically bureaucratic? Are all Latinos expressive and emotional? Of course not! More are probably so in these cultures than in others, but you are inter-acting with real people, not with a mass phenomenon.

One danger here is when cultures begin to believe too much of themselves and their own uniqueness. The Thais have a won-derful culture, awash in sophistication, esthetics, and depth. One of Omar's Thai clients recently asked him as he was interacting with his team, "Don't you find the Thais unique?" This client said this with considerable pride. Omar knew he further felt that even within the already very different Thais, his team was even more exceptional. This was part of the problem. This talented team was blinding itself to areas for improvement; they were being diminished by the arrogance of their own leaders.

Omar's answer wasn't a model of sensitivity. He said, "No, I don't find them unique." This Thai leader looked at Omar, ini-tially shocked. Omar said, "I think you have a remarkable culture [which is true], and I am often in awe of the grace and focus of the Thai people [also true]. But I've been fortunate to find many treasures as well as challenges in all kinds of cultures around the world. We need to help your team first face the challenges spe-cific to your organizational culture. To achieve this, we should indeed use the strengths of Thai culture, but we will also need the courage to take on some of the potential limitations of that culture for the global aspirations you have." As Omar got spe-cific with him, and this client saw that this input came from real commitment to his team's success, he relaxed and rallied. He also came to value Omar's counsel far more as a result.

So the problem occurs when we project conclusive expecta-tions on the people we meet based on general descriptions. We need to stay attentive and open, and let people teach us who they actually are. That is far better than us trying feverishly to get them into a "category" we've been told they should fit into.

Also, our decision on how much to adapt to and how much to challenge what we find has to be market based and outcome determined. Omar has worked with The Ritz-Carlton hotel group. They have won quality and productivity awards in Mexico, where people initially assumed this wouldn't be possi-ble because of the more laid back culture that is attributed to the locals there. Instead of capitulating to this generalization, The

Ritz-Carlton decided to draw on the warmth and hospitality it found there, but still aim for their same "Gold Standards" of service and customer satisfaction. While delivered with Mexican flair, the timeliness, efficiency, and responsiveness became as strong in Mexico City as at, say, The Ritz-Carlton Seoul (at which The Ritz demonstrated that Koreans could be as friendly as any other of The Ritz-Carlton's "ladies and gentlemen" in more traditionally outgoing societies).

Speaking of friendliness, realizing that it is a universal, not a possession of a few cultures, the award-winning Changi airport in Singapore mounted a "smile campaign." Although many people decried the artificiality of the approach, it worked! It worked because the natural friendliness of the Singaporeans was elicited, and the more taciturn (to the perception of those from non-Chinese cultures) facial expression common in that island evolved, instead of being reasserted.

Let us give another hotel example. Walk into The Four Seasons George V in Paris, and you will experience not only the epitome of French sophistication, but also among the friendliest staff you can imagine—this in a city reputed for snooty and almost dismissive service. Leadership is about drawing out and creating what you are looking for, not just taking a local temperature reading and adjusting your vision accordingly. Of course, you need to do this with sensitivity, but it should be *human* sensitivity as much as *cultural* sensitivity.

To make this even clearer, let's take two other examples of people who travel all over the world being triumphantly themselves. But because they care about sharing value with others, they are welcomed by all kinds of cultures and people. One is the Dalai Lama. Whatever one may think about the political disputes with the Chinese government that he represents, many admire his quiet courage and his radiant spirituality. We don't expect him to tell loud stories in New York, sing Irish pub songs in Dublin, or know the intricacies of an aboriginal wedding.

A very different kind of example is Richard Branson, the iconic founder of Virgin Group. From Virgin Airlines to Virgin Music and far more, Branson's Virgin brand is about both style and cheekiness. Branson himself exemplifies this. The free-spirited billionaire is a philanthropist as well as a daring adventurer.

He's always pushing the envelope (one of his current projects is getting tourists into space!). No one wants Richard Branson to become more timid in Stockholm, more pious in Rome, more communal and less charismatic in Beijing. No, people look to experience Branson, a true original.

Again, both these people are well aware of the world around them. They aren't lazy; they immerse themselves in other cultures and people. But they realize that the purpose of global interaction and global leadership, is to help change each other, in addition to adapting to each other. They exemplify and showcase what's possible. So should we, for our benefit and that of our clients.

Far worse than pigeonholing, even based on essentially sound cultural observations, is to succumb to stereotypes. Alan's fans in the U.K., who experienced his sold-out "The Strategist," never came expecting to see him speaking like David Niven (or even Rowan Atkinson), sporting a tweed jacket, and stepping out for a spot of croquet at tea-time. Nor will the packed house he'll be playing to as he reprises this workshop in Sydney be disheartened if he doesn't show his facility with throwing shrimps on the "barbie" (barbecue) or head off to do some surfing on Bondi beach to take the edge off.

So don't get overwhelmed by the minutiae of cross-cultural awareness touted in these aforementioned books. Go out and pace the people you encounter. Experience the cities and cultures of the world, and see what they evoke in you. Bridge from that to your own experiences and share back, so the learning flows in both directions.

But remember that ultimately what we are hired for as consultants is to help people change their perceptions and create better results, and to enable fresh possibility. It is not to reaffirm their current perceptions and paradigms. So while you learn where to leave the chopsticks and which hand to use, also challenge your clients and colleagues in valuable ways. That's why we're needed.

Then, let's come through for them. As we're doing so, let's let them teach us what truly matters to them personally and to their situation. We can then be meaningfully adaptive where needed.

That's good consulting, intelligent personhood, and insightful leadership. It applies everywhere, at home and abroad. Let's go with that, and keep the admittedly fascinating cultural generalities touted by "experts" as the elevator music they are in the continuum of true communication. Let's instead let real education and real experience light the way.

World tour

- We have to understand where we are and beware of prepackaged verities from dubious, often misinformed sources.

- If we understand cultural concepts and contexts, we can make our case undeterred by local evasive maneuvers.

- As we understand how others celebrate, we gain insight into their communication, their priorities, and perhaps even some of their passions.

- People are hiring us for our originality, distinctive expertise and ability. Let's share them!

Part IV

Distinctive Places and Sights

Chapter 9

Getting Paid

How not to accept 18 gross of native straw baskets (a true story)

All right, so let's reinforce our mission everyone: We provide value to improve the client's condition, creating a dramatic ROI and, in turn, receiving equitable compensation.

There will be a test in the morning.

"Receiving equitable compensation" has three key elements, as you can see:

- Compensation: This should be in the form of immediately translatable, liquid monetary instruments, viz. *money.*
- Equitable: the *money* should be commensurate with your contribution to the improvement of the client (see Chapter 7 on value-based fees), thus creating a "good deal" for both parties.
- Receiving: The *money* has to be in your possession—in your bank, in your pocket, in your delegate's hands, but not in your dreams.

Round up the usual suspects (normal obstacles)

Claude Rains shouted to a subordinate in the famous *Casablanca* scene, when pressed to find perpetrators, "Round up the usual suspects!"

We have similar "usual suspects" in extricating our fees from foreign lands. How bad can this get? The following is an absolutely true story (whereas, we point out, *Casablanca* was not).

When Alan worked for a Princeton consulting firm, there was an office maintained with alliance partners in Manila, reporting to the company managing director for the area in Hong Kong, who reported to Alan, who was responsible for all of Asia and the Pacific Rim. It was long known to be impossible to repatriate dollars from the Philippines to the U.S. (or to anywhere else, for that matter), so the only thing being done was to build the local bank account and invest in local infrastructure. (The Manila office had four copy machines, each one state-of-the-art.)

One of the co-founders of the firm decided that he would slice through this Gordian financial knot, and flew over to try to get the money. His first attempt, hiding US$20,000 in his cowboy boots, came to a sad end when he walked with such a limp that it became clear he would immediately be either arrested or hospitalized at Manila immigration. For that, it was only a small portion of the available cash.

What followed was one of the strangest episodes in modern consulting compensation. The co-founder decided to buy and to export goods to the U.S. that he believed he could then sell to recoup the financial investment. He actually purchased 18 gross (2,592) native, woven baskets, and exported them to Bisbee, Arizona, where he lived most of the year.

As some of you have guessed, these were immediately non-competitive with the Native American woven baskets that were available for just a few dollars throughout that area, and the entire lot had to be written off, purchase price, shipping, customs, and all else included.

Yes, this stuff happens.

You'll find that there are currency limitations in some countries. (Virtually every country has strict rules about physical monetary instruments being taken across the border, not that you should ever consider receiving cash or equivalents for any work you do.)

Here are the types of issues to be wary of and educated about. We'll deal with preventive and contingent actions in the following.

Global learning

Although there is a great deal of talk about pegging your fee to the best monetary unit in use, we advise you to use your own country's currency as your standard. You're in the consulting business, not the currency business.

Foreign exchange fluctuations

This is the killer. Not all that long ago, the Canadian dollar was worth about 70 cents against the U.S. dollar.[1] They are now on par. Not all that long ago, the British pound had declined to about US$1.25. It's now at US$2.00, and London is among the most expensive of the world's cities. The euro has recently made strong strides against the dollar.

However, in a day, or a month, or a year, or whenever, the dollar will rebound, and, not that long from now, it will be at a much different rate. Currency fluctuations are excellent reasons to be paid in advance, so that you know what you have when you have it. You're not in the currency speculation game any more than you're in the basket business.

Quote fees in your own currency to be paid at exchange rates prevailing on the day payments are due.

Economies change

Ireland was once in dreadful shape economically, but, as this is written, has one of the most vibrant, growing economies in Europe and beyond. African nations tend to ebb and flow economically as grants and foreign aid appear and disappear. Everyone predicted dire straits in Hong Kong when it was returned to China, but it is prospering as it always has.

A promise today, well intentioned, may be broken by unusual economic circumstances, which can include natural disasters (tsunamis in Thailand) and political turmoil (Kosovo declaring independence from Serbia).

Extensive delays

Funds must negotiate these hurdles:

1. Your client informs its accounts payable department to draw a check.
2. The client's bank is informed that it must process a payment.
3. You receive some instruments (check, money order, and wire transfer).
4. Your bank must "translate" the funds into the local currency.

This process is rife with problems and holdups (and we use that term metaphorically, as well). Banks are quick to debit accounts, but slow as molasses in January to credit accounts.

Vignette

Alan was owed US$25,000 by a Canadian client of long and excellent standing. Remember for the moment that Canada and the U.S. share a rather extensive border, and are quite friendly as these things go.

He was sent a check for US$25,000 in U.S. funds drawn on a Vancouver bank. The funds were deposited in Alan's bank, then promptly debited, pending collection. Three weeks later, with the funds still not available, Alan was told that the check—*in an age of electronic banking*—was sent, physically, back to Vancouver for collection, by way of the U.S. and Canadian postal systems (one worse than the other). The funds were to then be physically collected in a similar manner.

The answer was to explain this to the client, which promptly wired Alan the funds, which cleared in two days, and tried to place a "stop payment" on the check. It was too late, and the next day, Alan was credited with US$50,000. The client told Alan to keep everything as a credit toward future work.

Believe us, it seldom works out that well.

Changing economies, fluctuating currency, moronic policies, and inevitable delays can make collecting money a horror show. Happily, there are plenty of techniques we have mastered to help you help yourself to what you ultimately deserve. Collecting funds internationally is not for the faint of heart!

Terms of endearment (how to grease the skids)

There are two dimensions to getting paid internationally: Preventive actions against obstacles, such as those we've noted, and contingent actions in case preventive actions fail. In other words, you may have a great fire marshal and the "no smoking" signs are posted, but you'd still better have fire extinguishers and insurance.

Preventive actions

- Create a formal, signed contract, which specifies clearly what the payment amounts and terms are and is signed by your buyer.[2] This is not a "handshake" event. (Although oral agreements are considered binding contracts in many countries, proving that across borders and at great distance is not where you want to place your bets.)

  Omar now has clients who agree work with him verbally, receive an invoice, transfer funds on the basis of an email exchange, and then ask for a simple agreement after the fact to retain for their internal audits. Try this only after an established relationship and track record, both on your side for delivering results, and on their side for paying promptly.

- Always require a substantial deposit. Do not accept responses such as "It's not our policy..." or "It usually takes 90 days..." You need immediate commitment. Clients who don't pay deposits on time or as specified rarely make installment payments *or final payments* on time or as specified.

  Omar was told by an associate that in Europe, clients don't pay in advance. This was after three years of Omar having collected well over seven figures from various European clients, always in advance! It is amazing how resolutely we are often told either that clients won't pay value-based fees or won't pay up front, long after we've demonstrated that they will! If they won't, that's our fault, not theirs. It reveals more about the consultant than the client.

  Global learning

  Some organizations have a policy that requires any discount to be accepted. Therefore, an offer of a 10 percent reduction for full payment in advance would have to be accepted by your client. It's worth a try.

- Offer substantial discounts for payment in advance. Nothing beats having your fee in your bank.

- If you have an alliance partner (or you can establish your own local account), have the funds deposited in your local bank in local funds. That will speed payment out of the client's pocket into a neutral pocket. Then have the bank wire the funds to your bank at home. Creating a "middleman" actually speeds the process in this case.

  If anyone is wiring you funds, have them state clearly to their bank that the full amount must be received into your account, net of any local fees, taxes or withholding charges. These can otherwise add up.

- If you are dealing with a multinational client that has offices in your own country, explore to see whether the local entity can pay you. (If the headquarters is in your country, it's usually pretty easy.)

  Regional headquarters can also help here. Getting funds out of Bangladesh was a nightmare when Omar was supporting Maersk, the shipping giant. However, a credit note sent by it to its regional office in Dubai liberated the funds for local payment to Omar's partner in Dubai within 24 hours.

- Don't worry excessively about taxes. A saving of a few hundred dollars on taxes, depending on the payment venue, can easily be lost fivefold if it takes three times as long to get your money. Don't be penny wise and pound foolish, especially if the client wants to pay you in pounds.

- Minimize the number of payments. The more payments, the more the creaking wheels of bureaucracy have to turn and grind. (The more noticeable the payments become, and the more susceptible they are to unforeseen events.)

- Establish periodic payments at the beginning of periods (for example, 90 days of retainer work), rather than at the end. At the beginning, you can wait to begin work. At the end, you're completely vulnerable, work is completed, and you have no remaining leverage.

- Make all payment terms "due on receipt." Never invoice anything at "30 days net" or you'll have to wait at least 60 days. Alternatively, if a payment is due on April 1, send the invoice on March 1, so that the check can be processed appropriately.[3]

- If any form of payment is to be sent physically, provide your courier account number, and specify that it must go by overnight means, which you will pay for. (We favor Fedex as the most reliable of all such options, but the important thing is to provide for it. Also, waive signature requirements at your end, or ensure that someone can always sign for you in your absence. A delay of three days at the Fedex office three miles from your home is as much of a delay as when the payment is 1,000 miles away.)

Contingent actions

- Never discuss a late payment with a purchasing agent, accounts payable clerk, or anyone other than your buyer. Your opening phrase should be "We have a problem... " Deal solely with the decision maker. It is his or her project at risk, and he or she will have the clout to take extraordinary steps. (Even in a computer society, there is still such a thing as a "manual check.")
- Don't wait. If the payment is a day late, start to inquire. Cash flow is the heart and soul of our business.
- Get a tracking number. Don't accept that "Oh, we sent that on Friday... " Get the courier tracking number and find out exactly where it is. For a bank wire from your client, if there is a delay in the funds being credited after it says it's sent them, ask for a copy of the bank transfer advice. This is proof of transfer, which can be given to your bank for tracking purposes. We've found this removes any ambiguity on this front very quickly, and the actual status or date of transfer is then quickly confessed.
- Stop work. This is the ultimate contingent action. It is the most powerful leverage that you have. There is no ethical obligation to continue your part of the agreement if the client is abrogating its side of the agreement. This is why you want to move the preponderance of actual payment toward the front of the project.

As you can see in Figure 9.1, the sooner you are paid during the progress of the project, the more leverage you have (and influence, by the way) financially. The more you allow payment to be made toward the end, the less leverage you have.

By "terms of endearment," we mean that you must create a great relationship with your buyer in case you have to overcome these obstacles, and, more importantly, you must put in place terms that prevent them from occurring at all, because that is your safest position.

Expenses are expensive

You are due to be reimbursed for reasonable travel and living expenses while on the road, and reasonable office expenses when not traveling. First, let's define "reasonable" in terms of categories:

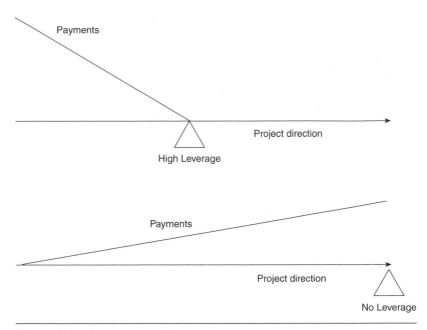

Figure 9.1 Payment and leverage

- air, rail, rental car, taxi, subway, limo
- hotel
- meals
- tips
- clothing laundering and cleaning (on extended trips)
- cost of materials (for example, if you purchase or print books for client use)
- currency exchange charges
- airport or immigration fees or taxes
- excess luggage penalties (for long trips)
- customs and duties charges for goods shipped
- local taxes assessed, for example VAT in the U.K.
- postage, duplicating, and copying when required while visiting

Here are "unreasonable" categories:

- recreation
- personal grooming (hair, makeup, shaving, manicures, and so on)
- copying, duplicating, postage, phone in home office

- health needs (massages, doctor visits, dentist, and so on)
- replacement needs (batteries, pens, beauty supplies, and so on)

We've talked about the need to travel well and treat yourself. In terms of expenses, here are "reasonable" guidelines for how much to charge:

- International flights of over five hours should always be charged at business-class rates to the client. If first class is also available (many times, business class is the only elite service provided), then upgrade from business to first on your own dime. Similarly, shorter fights should be charged at coach rates, but you should upgrade to business.
- Note that it's often cheaper to travel better. In other words, first class on many European and Asian trains is cheaper than flying business class, and also more efficient and comfortable. Therefore, a first-class train ticket is proper to charge for reimbursement when it is a cheaper alternative to flying.
- Limos are usually safer, cleaner, and more efficient than local cabs. It's fine to use these, especially for airport coming and going. Establish an international account with the likes of Carey International or Boston Coach, and you can make centralized reservations in most places.

Global learning

You have no obligation—nada, niente, nil—to obtain discount, nonrefundable, advanced, or other cheap fares. Schedules often change, and you don't want to be "hit" with penalty fees.

- You deserve a safe, quiet, and comfortable hotel. Brands such as Sheraton and Hilton are usually far better outside the U.S. than inside the U.S., for example. Ask your client for suggestions. Alternatively, if you choose to upgrade your hotel, charge the client a fair local business-hotel rate. If there are business grounds for using a specific hotel, for example, it's adjacent to the client office where you'll be most of the time, then your selection of that hotel should be no issue, irrespective of how deluxe it is.
- Always pro-rate expenses if you are visiting more than one client. It's easiest simply to divide them evenly among those visited, but if there are distinctions in terms of air distance or duration of stay, adjust accordingly. In other words, if you're going from Canada to Russia and then on to India, the Russian client should pay less of the airfare than the Indian client.

> ## Vignettes
>
> Alan was told by two clients he visited on one trip to Melbourne, Australia, that they would each have to have original bills from the airlines and hotel. No amount of explanation about the impossibility of providing two "originals" would work.
>
> He finally told them, "All right, I'll submit the original bill to one of you, but that one will have to pay the expenses for the entire trip."
>
> Within the day, they both decided they could expect copies of the bills to pay their pro-rated share.
>
> Truth is stranger than fiction. Omar was told by a U.S. client that he would have to provide original receipts for all expenses, including hotel and airfare; this after agreeing in the contract to pay expenses in advance! Omar asked it how it proposed he get it receipts in advance. After the email equivalent of some muttering, even this accounts department realized that it couldn't be a stickler in this instance. Afterward, the client mentioned what a relief it was not to have to deal with all the administrative follow-up and reconciliations. Omar assured him he was happy to oblige.

Now here is the key to getting paid: Submit expenses electronically at the conclusion of each month. (Make sure your proposal stipulates that "expense reimbursement amounts are due as actually accrued upon presentation at the end of each month.") Send a hardcopy by courier if the client has requested hardcopy receipts, unless scanned copies are acceptable.

Call your document an "Invoice and Statement" because some companies are fussy about requiring "invoices not statements," or vice versa. Be specific about any pro-rata amount or any exception. You don't want someone holding up your US$6,500 expense reimbursement over a US$25 questionable charge. Make sure everything is clear.

If you are not paid by wire transfer but by physical instrument, *consider including your Fedex account number or even a completed Fedex return envelope.* This will ensure the most rapid physical return possible. Don't kid yourself: If you are a true global consultant making seven figures a year, you may have US$20,000 or more of expense reimbursements due you at any given time. That can be serious cash flow, and you are losing money every day you're not paid because you're paying American Express, the travel agent and the car companies, *et al.* in the meantime.

Sometimes, during extended visits, the client will offer to provide an expense reimbursement check on the scene if you have a bill and receipts. If that's the case, come prepared. Be careful, however, just as you should be careful in accepting fees in this manner. The amount could exceed the level at which you'd have to declare the instrument at returning customs, which can create serious problems in terms of tax or even confiscation.

If you intend to travel in a manner more befitting your style, as we do, and always use first class, top hotel suites, extended-duration limos with drivers, and so on, then simply do this with your expenses: Translate them to a common denominator.

In other words, charge for business class not first class; charge for a Marriott-type single room, not the Four Seasons suite; charge for a local taxi, not the limo; charge for an average meal, not the gourmet experience at the five-star dining emporium. You get the idea. A good question to ask is: How do the client's top managers travel? Peg your actual reimbursement to the company's standard. Make sure that you are clear in your expense invoice about what you're doing, because your Marriott-level charge will be supported by a Four Seasons room bill. You need to tell the person reading it why that is and how it's to the client's benefit.

Some people like to include estimated expenses in their overall fees and not bill for expenses at all. That is "cleaner" in a sense, but there are these problems inherent in the approach:

- Inevitably, you or the client decides on more visits.
- Currency rates change against your favor, and the actual costs reduce margins.
- Your fee seems to be much higher than it actually is.
- You simply estimate amounts and frequency incorrectly.

We prefer the more candid approach: Your fees are for your talent and value; your expense reimbursement is for your travel and living. Keep them separate, but do speed both along.

What can also work factoring in all the preceding is to have your global assistant or local associate find out the hotel costs, and local transport charges to and from the airport, and estimate a reasonable amount for food and laundry or pressing (where applicable). You can then charge this in advance of these expenses being incurred, in a separate invoice from fees. Omar has done this for years, and will get expenses paid in advance of being undertaken by clients all over the world. For recurring clients, this is particularly straightforward. If you do this, it must be clearly stated and understood that unexpected expenses will be charged later. In practice, Omar only does this when they are significant. This way, there is a budgeted expense amount the clients are paying against. You are then almost never asked for supporting documentation because it has then become irrelevant.

The express lane

Cash is king. That is emphatically true across borders, yet the obstacles to collecting your cash, understandably, can seem daunting on an international scale. So we'll conclude this chapter by creating an "express" checkout lane of sorts. But you're going to have to pay attention and get into the right line.

We're going to discuss these as philosophical, process, and pragmatic needs, the three "p's" of profit across borders:

Philosophical

You need to emotionally grasp and internalize the fact—not the hope, but the *fact* —that we educate the buyer. If we educate the buyer that we are his or her peer, we will be treated as a peer and a partner. Partners don't allow each other to be poorly treated by their organization, by subordinates, or even by policies. They make things happen to create proper results.

Thus, a peer will help you shortcut bureaucratic processes, unstick dilatory payments, and end questioning of minor expense-report items. However, if you're not perceived as a peer, because you didn't comport yourself in that manner, then expect to be subject to the waits, rules, and penalties that every bureaucracy invokes on every "vendor" and "supplier," particularly those too far away to mount any kind of leverage or pressure.

Understand that this is a cash-flow business. Your bank will not accept promises of future client commitments for the mortgage, and the auto lease can't be paid with frequent-flyer miles. This is a business that provides cash that is fuel for your life and real wealth—your discretionary time. So you must make every effort at the "upstream" end of the system to maximize the raw material flow. No matter how much you like the buyer, love the project, are passionate about your methodology, see all kinds of future potential, and think the local shopping is sublime, *you are not going to be successful as a global consultant if you don't keep cash flow in mind at all times.*

Does that sound mercenary? It's not. It's simply sound business, and this is a business. Presumably, you want to make seven figures in this business. Trust us, you start with one figure that you make sure you collect, move on to two, then three—you get the idea.

> **Global learning**
>
> Manage your cash flow with all the discipline, focus, and creativity that you would use to manage your project. Is your cash flow "methodology" at least as good as your consulting methodology?

Process

Provide a motivation to pay early. That has to be in the *buyer's* best interest, not yours! In other words, the suggestion that the project can't be canceled or delayed by unexpected internal changes or external events is far more compelling than a mere 10 percent discount.

Follow up politely, professionally, *and firmly.* Never allow yourself to debate with low-level people. Your partner, the buyer, should be concerned if you are not receiving payments per your legal and ethical agreement. Don't wait. Use a date, perhaps two days after a fee is due, and follow up personally. Voicemail is best.

Always require (not request) a deposit of 50 percent if you can't obtain the full fee upon commencement. That has the pragmatic appeal of committing the client, paying for some of your expenses in advance, and providing leverage should you need it. (In the worst case, if you have to negotiate payment terms,[4] you'll be starting from a very strong bargaining position. If you begin with 10 percent as a deposit, you'll wind up with no deposit.)

Ensure that your proposal (or contract or agreement) is crystal clear on payment amounts, terms, and accountabilities. *Never* accept any amount of payment upon completion of the project, because clients will tend to draw projects out *ad infinitum*, buyers can change, and all kinds of events can intervene. More consultants lose revenue by being willing to accept payment upon conclusion than in any other way bar time-based billing.

If you can accurately and confidently estimate expenses—and don't panic if they are 15 percent off one way or the other—then do include them in the fees. This provides:

- the client with a single fee and a clear cap on all investment.
- fewer invoices and less appearance of continual charges.
- you with the latitude to travel and live in whatever style you please.
- you with the use of that money.
- less administrative and follow-up time for you.

Pragmatic

Ensure that you are funded sufficiently to withstand inevitable delays. Checks are lost. Dates are innocently missed. Paperwork is misplaced. Something is lost in translation. *Never rely on international payments for short-term cash-flow needs.* No matter how good you are, they are too unpredictable compared with the client down the block.

Use the road of least resistance. The fastest way to get paid is by wire transfer. Provide the key details for your clients, and request automatic deposits. You can track these online through electronic banking. (If your bank doesn't provide this, mark this page, put down the book right now, and go find a new bank.) *Note that you will need an international routing number, which is almost always different from domestic routing numbers.* You should carry this with you or memorize it.

It's also useful to use a bank near your home that can provide you with international services, not the least of which is currency conversion. Our banks can change dollars to euros or pounds, for example, and we always land in other countries with a pocketful of local currency for gratuities, a local newspaper, and so forth.

Consider using a local bank for deposits if you're doing a great deal of business in another country. It can ensure that the funds are no longer "stuck" in the client's system, and can readily transfer money to your home bank. However, you'll also have a small reserve locally for use as you need it for living expenses or minor investment in the business. *Check about local and foreign tax laws to make sure that this will be an advantage and not a net expense.*

World tour

- You want cash in the currency of your choice in the bank of your choice. Don't lose sight of that ultimate goal.

- The buyer is the key to cash flow just as much as the key to project success. Educate the buyer so that you are clearly perceived as a partner.

- Use local banking or alliance partners if they can help extricate and forward cash.

- Accelerate your payments to the front end of the project every time.

- Expenses also constitute cash, so be careful about ensuring their prompt and accurate payment or include them in the fees.

- Bonus: Never accept hand-made baskets if you intend to sell them locally in competition with other handmade baskets that cost less.

Endnotes

1. As we note in Chapter 1, the international monetary standard of measurement is the U.S. dollar, so we're using it for comparison here.
2. This might be part of your proposal used for the purpose. See Alan's book *How to Write A Proposal That's Accepted Every Time* (Kennedy Information: Peterborough NH, 2006).
3. Specifying penalties for late payment, for example, 1.5 percent per month, not only is tacky and unprofessional, but it doesn't actually hasten payment, and is never, ever paid in any case. Don't bother. It shows that you are used to late payments!
4. For the record, and even though it's not the subject of this book, *never* negotiate fees. If you must change a fee, then remove value from your project, or you're simply demonstrating that your fee was too high. See Alan's *Value Based Fees* for more detail. Negotiating payment *terms* can be acceptable in place of negotiating fees.

Chapter 10

The Human Software for Global Consulting

How to make the continuing sale to yourself

Of all the sales we'll be called upon to make, the seminal sale, the recurring sale, the most critical sale, is to ourselves. People assess us on many grounds, and certainly expertise and brand distinctiveness are among them. But we are judged most viscerally and subliminally based on *congruence* and *confidence*.

American essayist Ralph Waldo Emerson insightfully observed, "Who you are shouts so loudly I can't hear what you say." When we proclaim that we are one thing, but our mannerisms, our reflexes, our emotional balance, our physical vitality, our poise, the whole *gestalt* of who we are coming across as are broadcasting something else, we are perceived as disingenuous at best, flaky at worst. Such dissonance produces a feeling of incongruence, which reduces trust and unnerves people. Often, they won't even know precisely why, but the negative impact is produced nonetheless.

Nowhere is this more important than with the cultural and perspective differences that usually occur across borders.

One of the things we have to project beyond acumen is our confidence in our ability to help produce client outcomes and our passion for doing so. A clear deficit in our own lack of confidence, an unwillingness to be held accountable, any lack of clarity in the metrics we propose, any fuzziness about proposed ways forward that can emanate from perpetually second-guessing yourself, will create a corresponding lack of confidence in our clients. This is almost always lethal.

What makes energized confidence so compelling is that it reassures us that our experience and expertise will be optimally deployed, creatively tapped, and passionately brought to bear on the challenges at hand.

Making the continuing sale to ourselves is also important in the tissue of daily business building. We have to charge and recharge our emotional batteries as we build our brands and our relationships, recover from setbacks and mistakes, seek to project our value across geographical and cultural boundaries, and travel and seek to engage others in different settings and time zones.

We can intellectually persuade ourselves of the potential rewards of operating across borders in a global and increasingly interconnected world; we can deduce that it's worth consulting globally. But we also have to get to the point that we are confident we have the energy, the will, the desire, the stamina, the ongoing enthusiasm, and therefore the capacity actually to make it happen in a lucrative and sustainable way.

Making the ongoing sale: Self-esteem

Omar was dealing with someone who challenged the fees he was charging. Stupefied at the variance between Omar's fees and those of another consultant, this client said, "But Bob charges half of that!"

Omar replied without missing a beat, "Well, Bob is the best judge of the value of the work he's offering. I won't debate Bob's self-assessment. However, let's look at the value you're going to get from our work together."

The client laughed appreciatively, took an unromantic look at value rather than cost, and moved ahead.

These kinds of exchanges can sound arrogant and put people off if they are said with a prickly defensiveness that usually comes from insecurity. Or they can come across as reassuringly solid if they emerge from legitimate professional self-esteem.

Adjust this to local sensitivity. The need to avoid overly aggressive commentary, self-aggrandizement, or criticism of others is often paramount. But what goes on *inside your own head* is, thankfully for you, alone.

The first ingredient of self-esteem is making and keeping commitments to yourself. If you trust yourself when you say, "I'm going to do this," then by creating forward-moving intentions that are acted upon, you build your competence as well as your self-esteem.

One of Omar's clients had a health scare. His cholesterol level had skyrocketed, his blood pressure was way up, and he worked in a high pressure-cooker job as a global brand director for a beauty and cosmetics giant. In addition to revising his diet, he made a commitment to himself, his wife and his kids, that he would do 45 minutes of cardiovascular activity five days a week. So when Omar met him in Hua Hin, Thailand, for a conference, they agreed to set up a coaching session over breakfast at 7:30. Rohit had already been to the gym at 6:00. He arrived, glowing physically and emotionally, and was ready to go.

Some people manage best with an "all or nothing" approach. Rohit needed to baby-step his way there. He started with one morning, and kept adding to the commitment until he was where he wanted to be.

So it is consistent action, not intentions in the abstract, that builds our confidence and esteem. Similarly, Alan once shared with Omar that when he now contemplates new business ideas or initiatives, he assesses them by primarily selecting those that can deliver at least US$100,000 in income. In a similar vein, Omar and his company aim to cultivate client relationships that can deliver at least US$60,000 to US$100,000 per annum in consulting income.

The moment you make this choice and act on it, you have to create value that justifies that kind of paycheck. Everything you do, from your comportment, to the quality of your communication, responsiveness, alertness, and edge, has to reflect that "US$100,000" or, better yet, the overall seven figures you are seeking to earn each year.

Alan and Omar pretty much ring in those chosen numbers per engagement or consulting contract, but if you seriously embark on such an effort, and a particular undertaking or client brings you US$50,000 instead of more, hopefully your self-esteem will still benefit. You created value! You deployed your imagination, you created an intention, you conceived, you communicated, you acted, and you delivered. Each time you do, you help make the ongoing sale to yourself as well as to others.

The danger comes when we achieve certain results that are impressive, say a US$300,000 annual turnover, and rather than aim for the next rung of self-esteem or achievement, we accept this plateau. To be fair, if we do it consciously and knowingly, aware of the cost–benefit tradeoff, and on behalf of a life we want to lead, that's fine. But be careful otherwise not to be prematurely contented with levels of achievement that reflect our own torpor or lassitude, not what's really possible.

An associate said to Omar one day that he was worried about developing too much of an ego in this field. Omar challenged his presumption. If your ego is robust because of acknowledgment you've received from clients and colleagues who truly would know better otherwise, then don't "make yourself small," as Marianne Williamson warned. As she rightly suggested, us being "small" doesn't serve anyone. We are sometimes more frightened by the implications of earning and validating the self-belief of being a truly sought-after global expert who can run a seven-figure practice, than we are of a rut we've fallen into.

Alan often reports that when he takes strong positions publicly in his newsletter or blog, some people feel obliged to write to him and say he is being overbearing or arrogant. Omar has had junior consultants sent by associates to experience his conference sessions, who have returned saying, "Boy, he really is full of energy and ideas, and full of himself!"

Global learning

Confidence is an inside job and is infectious. It's a great thing to pass on. Its opposite is not something you want to be charging for.

Real arrogance, the type to worry about, is indicated when we either ignore or diminish others, or give ourselves kudos far in excess of our achievements in a self-aggrandizing way.

But these are instances where Alan has either stated a view based on experience, or has set out parameters of either privacy or engagement necessitated by being a public persona. For Omar, when galvanizing an international conference audience, he often has had to challenge pet paradigms, and be provocative enough to help generate alternatives to stale and failed options that are being repeated in that industry or marketplace. You don't do that half-heartedly or anemically. (We'll have more to say about the nature of feedback to welcome actively as opposed to that you should as actively shun later.)

The real impact both of us are after is improved results for our clients. When those are produced, then setting parameters or having a particular point of view (which in both of our cases is globally sought after and highly paid for) isn't "arrogance." It's simply acting on what we teach and demonstrating what we offer.

Happily, there are readily available brakes for what is truly unhealthy egotism. Namely: Responsibility and integrity, two other sources of self-esteem. Particularly when we consult globally, people are counting even more than usual on our professionalism, our code of ethics, our confidentiality, and more.

We believe that one of the fastest ways to build a reputation for coming through with clients to is make tangible commitments even if the client is seemingly satisfied with something vaguer.

We've had clients say, "So I'll get a note from you on this some time at the end of next week?" We'll reply, "How's Wednesday by close of business?" They usually respond very positively; we've become a source of clarity and greater precision in their lives. Then we'll get it in by Tuesday morning!

By volunteering precise commitments, and meeting or beating them, we build a storehouse of goodwill and reliability. Then, if for some unforeseen reason, we have to ask for some understanding or flexibility, it's almost always forthcoming with no issues.

But when we hold ourselves to a code like this (see the credibility habits we wrote about earlier), one of the byproducts is also a further blossoming of our own self-appreciation. We enjoy being counted on, and we count on ourselves to come through for others, and ideally ourselves as well.

Integrity is called upon in more taxing ways some times. Omar subcontracted some work in Asia. The delivery associates for whatever reason bombed with that audience. Angry letters were sent to Omar. Omar could have offered a part refund (they hadn't been incompetent, just disappointing), but instead offered additional value. He offered a day with him at a mutually convenient date or a commensurate retainer value to give the participants the ability to address the issues they reported had been superficially and inadequately handled by these presenters through emails, telecoms, and so on.

A note of appreciation was sent by the CEO for what he called this "high-integrity response." They opted for the retainer value, the participants got the coaching and input they were seeking, and the relationship with the larger parent company (the primary client) has continued to thrive.

Knowing he would make it right when the responsibility was at his end was necessary for Omar to be able to engage this client in the future with confidence. When you act in this way, then one of the other worries about contracting with someone at a distance (the fear of what recourse we would have across borders if something doesn't work) becomes immaterial. Your professional ethics and character provide the underwriting.

In short, to protect our own confidence and that of others we must *act consistently in ways that earn our own and others' esteem, express our responsibility and confirm our integrity.*

Rules for creating and retaining self-esteem across borders:

- Make and keep commitments to yourself and others.
- Communicate in ways to yourself and others that foster confidence.
- Although always with cultural sensitivity, express the points of view people are after all paying for, and don't let the "catcalls" from the gallery, so to speak, faze you.
- Always have backup and contingency plans, particularly when you have to demonstrate your ethics and trustworthiness.

Enthusiasm for the ongoing sale: Pick your friends

As we make our way around the world, one of the great pleasures of travel is the ability to pick up new friends. To us, this is far away from attending client events and empty socializing. Both of us try to avoid these mundane cocktail parties or compulsory dinners like the proverbial plague.

Some of that may have to do with our own particular psychological makeup. Despite having very active public personas, we are inherently social introverts who get far more of a "recharge" in intimate settings, with a book, or a bottle of wine, or sometimes our own muse. Other colleagues we know are actively energized by socializing at dinners and other occasions. They network in a very direct and personal way. We do too at times, but it takes far more of an effort for us.

More to the point, we find client dinners to be counterproductive in many ways, particularly during multiday events. For one, assuming a packed day already, the last thing we want is to continue the workshop or session in the evening. That inevitably happens because someone wants to pick up on a point we made, or share his or her own philosophy of life or business. Frankly, this can be depleting at the very time you're supposed to be recuperating. Second, multiday or not, after you've helped catalyze the group, this is a golden chance for them to speak freely, to catch up with each other, possibly to deepen some relationships. When we are in the middle, that is constrained, and our presence renders the evening inevitably more formal and stilted than it need be.

The exception to this is when you spend enough time with certain clients that you truly become friends. Then, the same conversations happen whether you're there or not, you don't have to be the center of attention, and you're quite content to enjoy the company and ambience, and hopefully the camaraderie, as quietly or as loquaciously as you'd like.

By picking your friends, we're encouraging you in various locations to create contacts, people whose company you enjoy, folks you can perhaps even learn some things from, and then to cultivate those relationships with the same care as any others closer to home.

Global learning

Global friendships help cultivate global outlooks and global connections and are a way to carry aspects of "feeling at home" with you. As has been so rightfully observed, home is where the heart is.

Omar hosted a dinner in Singapore, and was able to introduce a client and friend who manages real estate developments in Asia to another client and colleague who helps global companies establish operations in Asia, particularly in emerging markets such as Vietnam. It wasn't an evening of evident networking, just of shared good cheer. Certainly, follow-up invitations out for Singapore Chili Crab and a weekend hike in a beautiful nature reserve followed by a night of steak and martinis made the next visit to Singapore that much more inviting to look forward to. Having friends you look forward to catching up with and experiences that you expect to relish certainly help boost your energy, perhaps even your overall élan and confidence as you undertake your subsequent trips.

Global action point: Seek out relationships among natural networkers, influencers, those who can make things happen. Having that quality and caliber of relationships can give you not only emotional refreshment and pleasure, but perhaps also critical support should you need it. While consulting for The Ritz-Carlton years ago, Omar ran across an effervescent, hugely engaged executive in his sessions, Nanditha. Years later, she lured Omar to stay with the next hotel group she moved to, ensuring that he was thoroughly and warmly looked after. Over this time, Omar and she spent time chatting, and occasionally socializing, Omar became an unofficial mentor for her. When Nandi moved on to a regional sales position at another company, Omar was establishing a base in the Far East.

Nandi volunteered to help on her own time, given her enthusiasm for Omar's work. She volunteered as a local guarantor, helped open bank accounts, found a former Ritz-Carlton colleague to join Omar's team, and provided Omar with a virtually instant setup in Singapore. The years of friendship after the first meeting at the Ritz had never led Omar to suspect that one day, she would be such a wonderful and redoubtable enabler and ally. But when you sometimes least expect it, friends come through... and as we build such friendships, we build not only our enthusiasm but often, our capabilities in far-off places as well.

Global action point: It behooves us to partner with, befriend, and collaborate also with those who have distinctive talents, points of view, or abilities. Finding carbon copies of ourselves around the world isn't a great way to build a thriving practice or a fulfilling life.

Recently, a journalistic heavyweight, and one of the founders of modern-day conservatism (although he would have traced his lineage to Edmund Burke), William Buckley (who prepared the intellectual ground for the Reagan revolution), was being paid homage to by many current writers he mentored. Some of what they remembered was very telling.

Buckley was a grandiloquent communicator, who engaged in sharp debate with brio and a rapier-like wit. Yet he would often be found raising a champagne flute after the dialectical dust had settled with trenchant opponents, people like the economist John Kenneth Galbraith and historian Arthur Schlesinger, and long-time Democratic senator Patrick Moynihan (always referred to as "the gentleman from New York"). *New York Times* columnist David Brooks, who was given a job by Buckley after Brooks roasted him in an article for his occasionally haughty airs and lavish tastes, was astonished first that Buckley responded to being roasted wittily by offering Brooks a job. But Brooks rightly added, "Buckley had a great capacity for friendship."

When you can engage, occasionally bedevil, and frequently befriend such a constellation of opinions and outlooks and viewpoints, and never disparage those you disagree with, you build a true brand, a real standing, and arguably a healthy inner composure as well. The shrill histrionics of today's commentators are in stark contrast to this—and probably attest to the insecurity some people feel when their ideas are never tested, and when they're so unsure of themselves that they seek friendships as a preservative for their own dogmas.

Alan runs a highly sought after annual session called "The Odd Couple" with our colleague and mutual friend, Patricia Fripp. Patricia and Alan are endearing foils for each other. They have differing advice to offer on networking, how to prepare for speeches, the use of notes while presenting, and much more. Both are highly successful, both come across quite distinctively, both differ in everything from accents to style, yet their messages synthesize well, and there is great respect and fondness between them.

This has been a lucrative, productive, and recurring engagement that has been brand improving for Alan and Patricia Fripp. It would have been impossible, had Alan only befriended or delivered with people who agreed with him on every point, or came across with the same style as he does. Great opportunities within your own borders or across global borders are available when you can effectively and lucratively connect and partner with a broad array of talents, personalities, and styles. That said, the one thing you *do* want in common is fundamental values.

Opportunities for the ongoing sale: Pick your clients

Choosing our clients is not synonymous with choosing our friends, though there are overlaps.

To some extent, as our brand develops, we do need to be selective about clients. We may first impose some financial selectivity. We may opt to work for clients who have a certain magnitude of problem or need. Some consultants call this a "minimum check." If our fees are based on value delivered, then we may have a threshold before we are interested in taking a project on. Again, that's fine, as long as it's clearly communicated, and gels with our brand.

One of the tricks in picking your clients is to pick those with a solid track record for results and for driving execution, particularly those that others fear or pussyfoot around. These are the types that usually don't brook fools lightly, but readily become life-long fans of those who aren't cowed by them, who bring value, and who have the confidence to tell truth to power.

Omar recalls four such characters in particular. The nationalities and cultural styles ranged all across the map. One was Indian, another Belgian, yet another a Dane, and finally a South African. They headed local operations for their parent companies in Bangladesh, Vietnam, Pakistan, and Hong Kong respectively. Each was supposed to be suspicious of "soft" approaches. To them, these usually concealed mushy thinking. Omar was able to engage them as peers and quickly win their respect because he knew that fabled though they were for both their tempers and their results, when it came to engaging leaders relative to improving human performance, he had distinctive expertise they could use. The trick was always to link the improvement to results. No mush, no muesli, simply something they could take to the bank.

The depth of the relationships built and respect gained were demonstrated when the South African leader, Milton, asked Omar to videotape some role plays of effective and ineffective coaching to be shown at their global conference. Omar was then to facilitate a session based on these role plays. This was relatively early in Omar's career, and he quoted a fee accordingly. Milton sputtered, "Are you nuts? With the quality you provide and the work I expect you to do to make this really world class for us? Double it!" Few clients have told us our fees were too low. But we've each had the experience, and had our eyes opened by it.

Each of these leaders has since gone on to become a regional director or global CEO. Three out of four of them use Omar extensively to this day, six to seven years later. All are active references and good friends.

The benefit of picking clients for stimulus as well as value suggests three things to consider when undertaking an assignment. One, can it pay the fees I'm interested in (on a value basis)? Two, will I learn something from the work? Three, will working with this client improve my brand? We recommend aiming for 85 percent of client assignments scoring three from three on the above, and 100 percent of them scoring high on at least two of the dimensions.

Global learning

Our clients reveal a lot about us. Smart people make smart choices. We feel our clients should in choosing us. So should we in choosing them.

You will occasionally agree to do less remunerative work, say for a non-government organization, if it's work you find exciting or valuable on other fronts, and having done the work (for example, Omar's work with best-selling author M. Scott Peck's Foundation for Community Encouragement and for Oxfam) will be brand building. At other times, you may do slightly repetitive and somewhat dull work, when you're working with a top-notch company (this happened to Omar's company Sensei once with Microsoft) and the fees on a value basis are excellent.

Again, working with stimulating clients and demanding leaders will not only get you more credible advocates and referees, but will also once more increase your own inner excitement for the work, and further fortify your confidence and esteem. When you run with those who are in some ways faster and better than most, your own pace picks up, your own game gets better. As you respond, and demonstrate that you can positively affect them and their business, your own standards for yourself and your work rise.

Calibrating the ongoing sale: Choose your feedback

Nothing is more debilitating to energy and confidence, particularly as you're seeking to penetrate global markets, than unsolicited feedback, particularly from those ill equipped to offer it.

A client of Omar's demonstrated this very well. In a strategy session, this technology company's global lawyer had been

brought in to participate. He heard some verbiage from an offi-
cious senior manager, and challenged it. This manager said self-
importantly, "I am a Ph.D. in technology transfer."

Steve, the U.S. lawyer, said as gently and as genuinely as he
could, "Wow, that's truly impressive. But in this instance, what's
the point?"

The manager repeated himself more loudly, "I am a Ph.D. in
technology transfer." Steve said with no condescension, "Okay,
noted. I can't see any technology that we're trying to transfer
here though."

After a few more minutes, this manager abated, and the
dialog continued. Steve wasn't going to be intimidated by inapplicable credentials or a simple assertion of educational standing. Neither should you.

Both Alan and Omar eschew the "happy sheets" that are so
faithfully handed out after workshop sessions. We've both refused
to participate. We've instead recommended checking on impact
in the aftermath in terms of application. That's what we're interested in and so should the client be. Less interesting is whether
people unanimously enjoyed being jolted awake or constructively
challenged. We hope they were, but that has to be secondary.

People presenting often fixate on the few who don't respond,
thereby effectively ignoring the bulk of the room that is with you,
nodding encouragingly, and eager to gain insight or knowledge.
By seeking to convert the few cynics or critics, we give them
undue and undeserved power. We then link our ego to their conversion. That's ridiculous! We're not there to be elected to office.
We're there to help people improve their performance and effectively tackle their problems. When the bulk of your audience is
clearly ready and keen to do just that, then they deserve our
energy, our passion and our attention, not the carping cynics
who are often only looking to excuse their own inertia.

A business entrepreneur once said to Omar when he was
starting out, "Never ask people who haven't done it whether
your dreams are possible. Most people ask their Uncle Louie
about starting their own business. Louie has worked for the
same employer for most of his life for a pittance. He says you'll
starve and it's not possible. My suggestion? Find someone who's
done it and ask *them* if it's possible!"

Accept and invite feedback from those you respect, and for specific things you are seeking to improve. Don't, however, become an absorbent for everyone's point of view being dumped on you.

If you're a regionally ranked tennis player, you wouldn't let someone who plays casually on a few weekends rattle you after a tough match by saying, "I know what you were doing wrong." Apply the same principle as a consulting professional. On the other hand, as that tennis player working with a top coach, you should be aware that now you're *asking* for the input. In that instance, leave the defensiveness at home, and divert your passion to raising your performance.

Global learning

Just as we have to pick the right vitamins and minerals in the right amounts for our health (overdosing even on these isn't wise), so we have to pick the right people, those we can learn from, for feedback in targeted areas.

Progress is what matters

In Omar's recent book, *Liberating Passion: How the World's Best Global Leaders Produce Winning Results* (John Wiley & Sons, 2007), he discusses a technique called "the possibility focus." It is a way to protect the type of confidence and energy needed to build your consulting business globally.

At selected intervals, ask yourself what's gone well, what you've learned from it, what opportunities may exist as a result, and anyone you would like to thank for helping make it happen. When you do this, you can clearly map your overall progress: Things that are working and actions you are taking to continue and accentuate that trend.

As a follow-up you can always ask, "In what areas of my business would I like to be producing better results?" But the sequence should always be to first acknowledge what's succeeding, and then to consider what we wish to improve. That way, our energy is first lifted, we're more optimistic, and our standards for what is achievable are higher too. If we start with what's not working, we feel down and get sapped. Then if we try to ask what future-creating actions we may take, we're unlikely to find much creativity or will in ready supply.

Global learning

Always focus first on how far you've come and why. Start by feeling good today, and then you can shift focus to getting better and feeling even better from today onward.

Frequently map progress and forward movement. Also remember to practice the "attitude of gratitude." Grateful people are to some extent successful people because they optimize their assets. They "appreciate" things, and thereby increase their value. They don't take their health, their opportunities, their family, their friends, their clients, the wonderful diversity of a world brimming with opportunity for granted. We both recommend that you frequently "wallow" in your blessings as the best way to stir the desire and drive to increase them.

You make the continuing sale to yourself in part by acknowledging with gratitude and joy what the ongoing sales you've already made to yourself and others have already produced!

Global consulting may make more demands on our confidence, our energy, our resilience, and our responsiveness, both in terms of providing remote value to people faraway and in other time zones, or due to the inevitable wear and tear of travel. But it can also supply us with an even richer bounty of friends, experiences, learning, and memories than we could have reeled in otherwise.

And as we experience more, learn more, and are grateful for more, to some extent we also become more as individuals and as professionals. When we then come home, we bring all that with us. So our families, friends, and clients back home also get to participate in the value of our global experiences, and share in some of the benefits of our continuing growth.

World tour

- Action builds confidence. Earn your own confidence each day.
- Carefully chosen and well cultivated Friendships give us allies, renew our energy, and give us reasons to be excited to get out there.
- We have to also make sure we choose some clients we can learn from and who will challenge us to deliver at our best.
- Never let unsolicited feedback bring you down. Choose your feedback sources based on learning value.
- Pay attention to what's working, be grateful for all you've achieved, and always focus on the progress made.

Chapter 11

Life Balance

Enjoying the challenge

We spoke in the previous chapter about "taking a bit of home with you" as a way to continue to energize yourself, encourage yourself, and increase your passion and confidence while on the road. Moreover, we've alluded in earlier chapters to the efficacy of having favorite hotels, condos, and local bases. Not only will you get better service and exceptional support for all kinds of needs, you will also be emotionally buoyed when landing in a familiar haven, rather than in a sterile temporary base camp.

To add to this, and frankly to avail yourself fully of it, requires realizing that life is paramount. We both decry the artificial separation of "work" and "life." The insidious phrase "work/life balance" implies that there is work and *then*, when and if you can squeeze it in, there's life. That's absurd, and dehumanizing besides.

The reason to take on global consulting is to expand our profits, our horizons, our range of friends, and our constellation of interests, to give us more markets to tap in challenging times, and to make our lives richer and more interesting overall. You can't do that if you're segmenting life into artificial "work" and "life" compartments.

All of it is our life. We are the chessboard. Many pieces show up on that chessboard by invitation. We decide the moves to make with those pieces and the value and priority they each have for us.

Life balance in the global consulting context in particular requires balance in terms of time, family, emotions (which need to be flexed in innovative ways as we leave our usual moorings), mindset, energy and vitality, and the overall desire to be architects of a life we wish to lead.

Time balance

One of the first things we have to do in the midst of a hectic working and traveling schedule is to quarantine time for those particular trips, experiences, or interactions that are most crucial to us. Alan has his annual summer trips to enjoy the many exquisite pleasures of Nantucket and Cape Cod, Omar his annual theater pilgrimage to the exceptional Shaw Festival in the historic Canadian town of Niagara-on-the-Lake. These are blocked and booked by us respectively each year in advance.

You may have favorite weekends you want to carve out: for Alan, New York visits to meet with his kids and catch up on the latest Broadway shows and Carnegie Hall concerts; for Omar, walking trips through the countryside and cuisine of places such as Provence to clear the mental and emotional decks.

Identify and carve out these times actively. Place them in your calendar first, and work around them. Subtract them from your calendar and guard them from encroachment. If you take these away from your booking schedule, you have two benefits.

First, you realize vividly that the remaining days are what you have available to hit your financial targets! When Omar first reduced the number of days he was willing to work (a shocking concept to him at first!), he realized he had to raise his game, his value proposition, his caliber of clients, and his capacity to deliver outcomes with less labor intensity, to achieve *more* net income with *fewer* working days. Doing this really stimulates your creativity, and potentially kicks loose overdue innovation.

Remember that wealth is discretionary time, a favorite saying of Alan's, and you don't want to allow even too much money to eviscerate your true wealth. The both of us could make more money, but at what cost to our wealth? This is critical in global work.

Second, because you want to add more such experiences, you realize you need a business model that allows you to earn income even while you're enjoying them. So if you're facilitating a leadership summit in Manchester, England, and decide to take the long way home, by taking an extended weekend in Rome (dubbed "the Eternal City" for good reason), it's nice if people are buying your products, signing up for your upcoming offerings, asking for input that you can take a focused hour and respond to, or if you on the flight back write a key chapter for a book or an article for a journal that will add to the value of your brand.

Global learning

Without balancing how your time is applied, you can't thrive personally or professionally. Life is time. Squander one and you squander the other.

This airplane time can be a wonderful sabbatical in itself, as long as you travel in first class or premium business if that's what's available, as we've advised. You can catch up on movies. Chat with a loved one who's traveling with you (more on this when we discuss family balance) over a glass of champagne or carrot juice (depending on whether your palate or immune system are more in need that day). Use the in-seat power supply to respond to emails you've downloaded before you boarded so when you land you're not distracted. Make progress on good books or journals. Catch up on some extra sleep. Meditate to soothing music, or perk yourself up with something musically more rousing. You get the idea.

Of course, travel also creates time impact because we often change time zones. You can deal with time zones in several ways, so you don't spend heavy travel months completely zonked, dysfunctional, and feeling perpetually suboptimal. First, keep hydrated during travel. That's a big part of jetlag. Omar's wife Leslie swears by homeopathic "no jetlag" pills. Use what works for you here. Certainly, move around periodically. Stretch every so often. When you land, hit the gym if you can, because the oxygen quality on most planes is dodgy (as our British friends would say). Aerobic workouts send oxygen-enriched blood pumping to the brain and throughout our body. A walk exploring where you've landed might be even better. Throughout the flight, try to sleep as close to the new time zone as you can.

Alternatively, if you're only going to be away for a few days, you can use a trick that Mark McCormack (who was a business CEO and best-selling author) used. When landing in Japan, where night was literally day for him relative to U.S. time, he would adopt the following regimen. He would sleep enough on the flight over to Japan, but not too much. Accordingly, he was tired enough to sleep at night upon arrival. Jetlag and his slightly addled biologic clock would usually wake him several hours later. He had planned to capitalize on that.

Having gone to bed around 11:00, he would awaken at 3:30. He could "just" catch people back in his office in the U.S. He'd have a workout, order some coffee, and work until about 7:00. He'd schedule a breakfast meeting, and continue working until 12:00. After a good lunch, he was usually tired, and would nap from about 2:00 to 4:30. He'd then get up, take a walk, meet colleagues and clients for drinks and dinner. He reported that for a three-day trip, he never got fully out of the U.S. time zone, and was able to function at high levels of effectiveness, and return home without being devastated for several days. Experiment, and apply a regimen that works for you. Don't be a victim of seemingly inevitable and extended down time.

We both love fine wine, but there is a strict limit to our indulging on airplanes, since it creates dehydration and sleep problems (and there is no "fine wine" anyway at 38,000 feet).

It's not always plane travel. Carefully consider, in terms of your life, time, and energy (all inextricably interlinked, of course) how best to get from point A to B. Omar was in Copenhagen and had to get to Marseille by the next day at noon. Having found very poor flight connections to Marseille from Copenhagen, it was simpler to fly to Paris after finishing in Copenhagen, and overnight there in comfort, and then to take the excellent French TGV trains (when not on strike, they are a stunning example of what national rail travel should be) in the morning. He arrived feeling relaxed and pampered, rather than surly and stressed.

Once, when Omar had to finish with a client in the hill country of the Philippines and make it to the airport in Manila the next day for a 5 p.m. flight to Canada, he chose to arrive in better shape and have a few hours to recuperate. Instead of an arduous eight-hour coach ride to Manila, he booked a helicopter, which whisked him there in an hour. He then had four hours to relax, respond to emails, get a massage, and have lunch. Yes, it cost US$4,000 for the helicopter. But there were three colleagues who shared the ride, it saved seven hours, and both sets of clients benefited from Omar's greater energy and alertness.

The work was remunerative enough that paying these expenses wasn't painful... on the contrary.

(Until they discontinued it, Alan had more than 500 air miles on the choppers connecting Kennedy, LaGuardia, and Newark airports. Consider the fact that the trip was about six miles, and you'll see how much he relied on them.)

You can sit clogged in Hong Kong traffic between Kowloon and the Island, or you can take the atmospheric Star Ferry, and watch the evening lights come on across the magnificent Hong Kong cityscape. During the day, if needing to make the journey in about five minutes, the excellent subway system is worth figuring out. While not a "luxe" trip, you can make it from a wonderful lunch at the Peninsula to a client's office near Pacific Place in about ten minutes. (First class on the Star Ferry is about five cents more than "coach." We both splurge.)

So, as we've said, try to pick intelligent times for commutes, and investigate different modes of travel (sometimes it's speed, sometimes it's convenience and comfort that are paramount). Find ways that optimize your time, comfort, and convenience.

Finally, when you're away, messes you've left behind tend to prey on you. The last thing you want to do is to be responding frantically to urgent calls, or fending off irate colleagues, or absorbing a family member's ire because of something you've left undone. Periodically review messes in your life, defined as recurring things that leech your energy, attention, and confidence. Some are surprisingly trivial. For example, not having recurring bills on autopay through e-banking, or not having credit cards with adequate balances for overseas travel (with the card issuers being informed you're on the road, because some "freeze" your account allegedly "for your protection"), and so on. Other messes may be more substantive; for example, having a poor website, and consequently having to arrange to send physical documentation in reply to all inquiries; or not having a way to get messages to you, so you're left having to placate someone you've ignored for days; or not having scheduled regular check-ins with clients who, for whatever reason, choose your days away to become uncomfortable and demand an update.

Identify your biggest time wasters, non-value-adding activities, and energy drains. Go to war on at least the top three recurring ones each quarter. As you simplify your life, remove such offending clutter, and streamline your overall support processes, you'll be liberated to enjoy your time at home and on the road. You will also focus your attention and energy on delivering results and earning the corresponding high-value fees that go with those results, rather than depleting yourself putting out unnecessary fires.

Family and emotional balance

Just as you can take a bit of "home" with you when you travel, you can do likewise with your family. Don't get carried away, we're not suggesting that you start families wherever you go! We mean you can structure your business and your life so that family members can contribute to your business and can often travel and experience the global stimulus with you.

Maria is a key presence in Alan's business. Readers of Alan's monthly *Balancing Act* and his books get to know Maria very well. Maria is also an active presence in Providence, contributing to many local organizations and community initiatives. Yet at a recent session run by Alan, one of the extras for people signing up early was a dinner hosted by Maria, where amusing "Alan stories" were part of the menu for the evening. On many occasions, Alan and Maria do travel across the globe together, racking up air miles and wonderful shared experiences. (As this is written, they are planning an Atlantic crossing in the largest suite of the *Queen Mary 2* later in the year, followed by two days of client work in London, and then a week's jaunt around Italy.)

Omar's wife Leslie is his business partner, so she travels on most assignments and Leadership Journeys with him. Therefore, he doesn't have to dash to head home each weekend. If they finish a session in Vietnam on a Thursday, and have an engagement in Bangkok on a Tuesday, the question is, "Where do we want to spend the weekend?"

Omar's clients appreciate Leslie's support facilitation and her working with their team to oversee critical details and arrangements. She is also a safe harbor for client team members who want an empathic ear. Omar is invariably asked, "Leslie is here with you, isn't she?" (As this is being written, Omar and Leslie have just spent a month on rewarding client work and rejuvenating personal time between London, Dubai, Phuket, Penang, Bangkok, Singapore, Hanoi, and Athens, before returning home to New York. During this trip, Omar's parents also came out to spend some time with them in Singapore—a wonderful month of professional and personal balance.)

Ron Kaufman, the Asia-based customer service specialist, and his wife Jen have adopted Omar and Leslie's model. Bob Urichuck, whom we wrote of earlier, has used his global sales consulting practice to give his son and his wife, on different occasions, round-the-world experiences.

Clients purchase value. When your brand incorporates some of your key relationships, your close relationships are accepted and welcomed wherever you go.

However, we have to use our judgment in what's appropriate. If they're there on that occasion socially, clearly you won't have them attend a strategy session. On the other hand, if capturing commitments and following up on client actions are part of the service experience you're offering, and your spouse is intrinsic to them, showcase him or her with pride as the business partner he or she is. If he or she is highlighted in your writing and speaking, then people will be keen to meet him or her. You then don't need to "explain."

However, even if a family member is present at a time when you are delivering client value, needless to say, your focus and attention have to be 100 percent on the client outcomes. As long as this focus isn't compromised, we've never known there to be an issue.

Your ability to leverage this is only limited by your imagination, initiative, and will. One of Omar's associates took his daughter along when he was conducting a series of marketing sessions in Sydney. He bought his teenage daughter a ticket, she shared the room with him, and she had the days to "be a teenager" in Sydney, and the evenings with Dad, which gave them both time together they were seeking. They came back via Singapore and Dubai, where he stopped in for client meetings, and global consulting became a mechanism for a very special father/daughter trip of a lifetime.

Global learning

Help family members prepare to savor deeply what they are going to experience. What a shame to be at the sight of the *agora*, below the Acropolis overlooking Athens, where Socrates taught his younger pupils, and have no idea what that signifies.

Your own emotional balance is relevant here too. There's no point having family around if you're a personal emotional wreck. Here are some ways you can keep your own emotional tank full as you make the world your consulting oyster (*"Why, then the world's mine oyster, Which I with sword will open,"* from Shakespeare's *The Merry Wives of Windsor*):

- Create your own list of life's pleasures. Actor George Hamilton wrote a little book called *Life's Little Pleasures*, in which he describes certain (for him) exemplary occasions and moments. An example is being in a hot tub in Aspen after an afternoon of skiing with someone you want there with you, with a bottle of champagne being chilled in the ice bank next to you. Another example is luxuriating in bed on a Sunday morning with freshly squeezed orange juice, warm bagels and lox, *The New York Times*, and a loved one beside you. Yet another is a spa treatment, then settling down in a luxurious robe by the fire, with a great bottle of wine, a cigar, and a good book. You get the idea! Create some of these wherever you go.
- If you're with loved ones or friends, don't just inflict what you want to do on everyone. Poet Khalil Gibran said, "Let there be spaces in your togetherness." He was right! You don't have to be grafted at the hip even if you're traveling together. Yes, it's wonderful when you can adapt for each other, and be a convivial and gracious companion (without acting like you deserve a martyrdom certificate and souring the other person's enjoyment). Equally, it's fine to let each other indulge in at least some pleasures that aren't necessarily shared.
- Realize that the final freedom is choosing our attitude. Victor Frankl wrote an extraordinary book entitled *Man's Search For Freedom*. In a concentration camp, he and fellow inmates discovered that while some devolved into beasts, others shared their own scant food and emotional comfort with others suffering still more. They even found some guards who regarded them with at least a trace of humanity, and even snuck them some extra food. Frankl observed that he learned something in that crucible that no one who was there could ever debate. Namely, the one thing no one can strip away, the final human freedom is the freedom to choose our attitude. When we relinquish that, we give a fundamental part of ourselves

away. Certainly, don't be passive when you can change things. When you can't, pick an attitude of graceful acceptance. The only one who suffers otherwise is you.

Global learning

Be aware of the time you waste indulging unproductive "toxic" attitudes, such as bemoaning that life isn't fair. Consciously shift to the "tonic" of focusing clearly on what you do want and on how to move progressively in the direction of getting there.

- We are not entitled to be obnoxious just because we may come from a more affluent part of the world. The Golden Rule is the common wick in all religions, and is fundamental to what Aldous Huxley called "the perennial philosophy," those ideas shared in common among all civilizations and vibrant cultures across geographies and time. Some less outspoken cultures may absorb our outrage, but you won't get cooperation, and you may inspire the very enmity you don't want when in someone else's country seeking help. You can be firm, even adamant, while remaining respectful.

- We all deal with stress. Stress is not the same as pressure. Pressure is an objective fact. Two people in the same traffic jam, heading for the same meeting, will often respond very differently. One may break out in road rage, yell and threaten. Another may make a phone call and apologize, turn on a classical music station, take some deep breaths, and relax. The external stress or pressure are identical, the experienced pressure or internal stress for these two individuals is very different. You can always choose to take better care of yourself, or at least the best care of yourself possible in every situation. If, indeed, we can choose our attitude, then always choose the one that best serves you in every situation. If you fail, smile, yell it out if you must, then dust yourself off, and start over.

- Cultivate not only the extravagant "little pleasures" that Hamilton mentions, but those everyday things that increase your joy in being alive. Amplify whatever things make you emotionally grateful, joyous, and vibrant, and locate some of these to engage in while traveling too. These should be things you can do more often, wish you did more often, and now intend to make more time for. It may be a dark chocolate gelato, a walk on the beach at sunset, a picnic with supplies from a local gourmet deli, enjoying a local delicacy, a hike through a local park, browsing a favorite book store or art gallery, playing a game of tennis, catching the sun's rays by a pool, having a special date with dear friends in an exotic setting such as Buddakan in New York, Les Trois Garcons in London, Ukai-tei in Tokyo, Felix in Hong Kong, Al Qasr in Dubai, or Villa Gallici in Provence, having "movie night" in your hotel room with popcorn, or taking a fun and different tour (such as the ghost tours in Edinburgh or the night safari in Singapore). Pick your readily replicable turn-ons when you travel too, and go for them!

Mental balance

William Osler gave Dale Carnegie a famous injunction to trot out relative to keeping worry at bay. It was to live in "day tight compartments." In other words, seal off the dead yesterdays you can do nothing about, leave off paranoid worries about unborn tomorrows, but put all your passion and energy into living effectively, imaginatively, and passionately today. That doesn't mean don't plan. It means don't worry. Planning *is* doing something today. Worrying isn't.

If we give ourselves a vivid intention instead of overwhelming worry, we get another boon. Our brain filters out most of what it perceives. We'd go stark raving mad otherwise. What it lets in is an amalgam of what we need to function and our own interests. So a visual artist will "see" more than either of us will on a walk through the same park. When we buy a Lexus, we suddenly see them everywhere. So we have filters. We can either "magnetize" our own mental filter to find evidence of worry, decay, and downfall, or to look at the world as raw material for the achievement of our aspirations.

Alan and Omar both write monthly newsletters. So the vexing and frequently absurd things we all experience now become raw material for entertainment and edification, not only for us but also for our many thousands of readers.

When speaking of 3M, it is often noted that both the Post-It and Scotchgard came into being while scientists were trying to invent something else. But charged with 3M's then legendary zeal for finding solutions to everyday problems, when something unexpected happened, they capitalized on it, rather than shunning it for not being what they were after.

There is a Zen saying, "When the teacher is ready, the student appears." What is probably more true is that when the student is ready, they see the teacher that was always there *everywhere*. So choose carefully what you're on the look-out for. "Seek and ye shall find" is a perceptual truth too.

Here are two more tips on mental balance. Many times as we encounter obstacles or challenges, they are simply asserted and assumed by others. Don't settle for that: Probe, check assumptions, verify facts.

We've said we recommend sending luggage ahead of you if you have tight connections or are just too laden with things in hand.

Omar sent on a suitcase to Toronto. It was held up at customs. Omar contacted DHL because the suitcase had been sent from Dubai, where DHL is much more active than Federal Express (experience has since taught that FedEx is far better at customs clearance arrangements in North America, the two are competitive in Europe, and DHL gets the prize in Asia). Omar asked DHL to hire a clearing agent if necessary to get the bag released. It reported that Customs wanted to open the bag in the presence of the passenger. Omar patiently explained that a clearing agent is a legal surrogate if employed. That's what one does! Though one was hired, the clearing agent too said Customs had a question for the passenger, and in his experience, that meant a personal appearance.

Omar pressed him on what the question was. By this time, everyone had assumed there was a problem with the bag. When Omar finally got through to Customs himself, the agents said they just needed the combination to open the lock! They hadn't even looked inside! The combination had been given to DHL, which had neglected to pass it on.

It then took five minutes (after the bag had been languishing for two days) for Customs to do a perfunctory check and release the bag. All this because DHL and the clearing agent used their own pet assumptions as to why Customs usually holds a bag without even calling and asking what the real issue in this instance actually was.

Global learning

Darwin's theory of natural selection is not really about "survival of the fittest"; but about the thriving of the most adaptable. Mentally, it behooves us to get on this evolutionary track!

Many times we are told something can't be done and we ask "how do you know?" So often, it turns out what's taking place is just rampant assumption mongering. So always ask for evidence, always check, always generate alternatives, always ask possibility-rich questions (even simple ones such as, "Okay, if you can't do what I've asked, what else could you do for us instead?").

Also choose your words carefully to maximize attention and responsiveness. If you're well known, state your name first, your most critical request next, and then any backup information. If you're calling your travel agent from Peru, don't say as hear she picks up the phone, "May I speak to George?" You'll then end up being put on hold with no one in a particular rush to get to you. Instead say, "This is John Roberts, calling from overseas, George is my personal account manager, and this needs immediate attention. Thank you."

At a hotel seeking a later checkout, don't call and say, "What is your checkout time?" You've then gotten them to state a time they now may be reluctant to back off from. Far better to call and say, "This is Jan Fulton, I'm in one of your club floor suites. My flight isn't until 8 p.m. I know your usual checkout time, but can you improve on that for me please?" You probably won't get an 8 p.m. checkout, but you'll usually do better than 12:00.

Whatever the situation, ask as though you expect help, allude to your custom or patronage of that establishment or service where appropriate (in an appreciative manner, not officiously), and ask an open-ended, possibility-inducing question. You'll get more help and better solutions more of the time than you might imagine. Your life, time, peace of mind, enjoyment, and energy will be the beneficiaries.

It's a great idea and a habit of the both of us to learn and record the names of key people in hotels, restaurants, and service establishments we frequent. Contacting a key manager, or even mentioning the name and your relationship, tends to turbo-charge the responsiveness you can expect.

You'll also heighten your own mental and emotional wellbeing and that of others if how you verbally frame things opens doors rather than shuts them—at least with clients, allies, service providers, friends, colleagues, and, of course, loved ones.

When a client makes a request that you can't accede to, offer options that show you're truly trying to help. Omar was asked to present in Jeddah, Saudi Arabia. The visa takes three or four business days. In the three weeks between the request and the day in question, he wasn't going to be at home for three or four days at a stretch. Instead of saying no to a very deserving and anxious client, Omar said, "I can't get a visa for that day unfortunately. You can shift your session to the neighboring country of Bahrain, where many of your meetings are held anyway. No visa is needed for U.S. nationals and those with businesses in the Gulf region. I can otherwise get two of my associates to deliver, based on a design that you and I agree, on the date and location you've indicated. Or the next time I can do it personally is the following month, based on calendar availability and visa-processing times. Which works best for you?" This was the kickoff for what turned out be a US$120,000 contract, two of Omar's top associates conducted that session, and the client was grateful rather than being annoyed or disappointed.

Our job is to generate options whenever possible, and accept what must be otherwise. As the famous prayer reminds us, we need to seek for the courage to change what we can, the serenity to accept what we cannot, and as much as anything, the wisdom to know the difference.

Energy balance

Finally, it all comes down to energy, the *élan vital*, our lifeforce. It is best to have recurring energy rituals. Managing our energy is even more important than managing our time.

The first energy rituals have to do with physical vitality. Alan has written of his discipline of going to the gym three mornings a week and then rewarding himself with a favorite cup of coffee and a feeling of personal achievement.

Alan uses a personal trainer three times a week, but gives himself permission not to work out when he travels. His trainer is fine with that, and the rigor or the training is acceptable in light of the "vacations" from it.

Omar has gotten into half-marathon walking. So the energy ritual when in New York is three 10 km walks a week through a mapped route in Central Park, a 7 km route through Hyde Park and Kensington Gardens in London, a 5 km loop (time seems to dwindle as he heads east!) in Singapore's Botanic Gardens early morning before the torrid humidity hits, and so on.

Omar had another client who had an energy ritual that helped him stay in overall balance. He pretty much ate what he wanted for dinner, but had a healthy breakfast, went to the gym at lunchtime, and had a sandwich or salad at his desk. For him, the tradeoff was worth it. Equations are as various as people. Find and apply yours.

Everyone has different sleep needs too, and this clearly relates to energy management. One of Omar's clients does an hour on the bike and elliptical machine each morning at 5:30 so he can have breakfast with his kids before school at 6:45 after a shower. He sleeps by 11:00 p.m. and says he's learned to "sleep fast and deep" as a result. Find out what works for you and get enough sleep, but not too much. Our body is made up of moving parts designed to... well, move!

It also helps to structure your work, particularly when on trips, keeping in mind what you know about your own productivity. Some people work best going full throttle for many hours and then completely switching off.

For most, productivity experts tell us it's better to rest before you get tired. Rather than waiting until you can't go on, which means you've switched out of "creative" mode into a mechanical fatigue for some time, take more frequent, shorter breaks. That way, you're in creative mode more of the time when working, and you can enjoy your recharges more too, because you're not combating burnout or pervasive fatigue.

Years ago, when Omar ran a Leadership Journey in more stable times in the mountains of Pakistan, an overly keen HR director insisted that the leadership team climb one of Pakistan's smaller peaks as a sidebar to the journey. Again, this was before Omar decided the flow of the journey would have to be fully in the control of his team. Since a Leadership Journey is to expand paradigms and deepen relationships, not to demonstrate your physical bona fides, this was a bit much. But an important insight was picked up.

It was an arduous three-hour climb taking people to 8,000 feet. The guides hired were very experienced mountaineers, who did glacier climbing in their spare time, and were years later part of rescue attempts in the mountain areas after a devastating earthquake. They couldn't understand why these young, seemingly fit executives were heaving and spent every 15 minutes.

Finally, the lead guide told everyone to walk much more slowly, so they wouldn't get tired. He said, "Walk at a pace you can breathe: One step, one breath." Initially, this seemed monotonously slow. But the group started to enjoy the climb, and made it up within the three hours. They rested before they got tired, but they also moved at a pace that allowed them to make real progress, but in increments they could handle.

We both are believers that energy and ability can be extended, but in reasonable progress-producing chunks. Total immediate metamorphosis is unhealthy, unlikely to succeed, and unnecessarily destructive of our pleasure and joy in life, as well as our ultimate achievement. Instead of being excited and stimulated, we will likely be demoralized and dejected.

Not all energy rituals are physical, of course. Another client of Omar's in Vietnam had to work at his office most days until 6 p.m. He then came home, and read something utterly unrelated to his supply chain responsibilities to unwind. Once the kids were in bed, he and his wife shut off all the phones, opened a bottle of wine over dinner, and had an uninterrupted hour and a half each evening to reconnect and enjoy each other's company. He did this each night he was at home, and despite his schedule, it was marvelous. When traveling, he went out to eat with a good book, and using Skype (which we wrote about earlier) made a free 30-minute call to his wife when time zones permitted either late at night or early in the morning.

So whether it's a massage, some tai chi, some reading, catching up on your local papers online, taking in a comedy act or local performance you enjoy, which unknots your stress, create some energy rituals on the road too (these may not be the "joy producers" we spoke of earlier, but seek them instead as revitalizers)—things that allow you to tank up your vitality and spend your working hours creatively focused.

Our clients pay us for our acumen, our engagement, our alertness, the vital application of our faculties. Bring that to the table, not a burnt-out husk. No one is interested in our exhaustion.

One of Omar's clients said recently after a particularly challenging transition to a bigger role, "You're one of the people in my life, who when I see them, pick me up, and make me feel better." Omar has worked with him and his team on trenchant

Global learning

Move in the direction of your aspirations. Don't expect instant results. When Honda Corporation first really took off, the business press called it an "overnight success." The relatively young Mr. Honda is reported to have said in reply, "It's true, but it took me my whole life to get to that night."

business issues. But if this feeling was also produced, it was an excellent bonus!

Making a life

Life is what it's about. We're ultimately not trying to make a living, but to make a life. That has to do with how we choose to contribute to communities or causes we believe in (and finding some of these overseas is a splendid way to expand our life interests), the things we wish to learn and understand, experiences we wish to enjoy and gain from, colleagues and friends we want to engage and be enlivened by, and a life we've created that allows us to make the most of our time with those we love, and to spend as little time in unprofitable habits and self-defeating emotions and outlooks as possible.

Our life is not about how we compare with someone else. There is a reason for the gift of uniqueness. Never to investigate that uniqueness, fulfill it, make it a part of what we offer are sad.

Economies rise and fall, and cycles abound globally. Those who innovate and do so on a global scale, have a great chance of riding these currents to increasing levels of success and satisfaction. So we need to both be a perennial work in progress and to accept who we are today... with appreciation, not resignation.

Being emphatically ourselves, imagining and inventing a life we want to lead and we take full responsibility for, is the basis for an extraordinary experience. That extraordinary life we argue can and should include extraordinary success. But it must be more than economic success. Alan has said discretionary time is the real wealth. Using that discretionary time as ardently and as meaningfully as possible from your own perspective is what life balance is all about.

Global learning

The French call it "*noblesse oblige.*" It means that to those to whom more is given, more is expected of them. As we gain more, if we are healthy, we will seek to give more as well. One way to give is to locate, cultivate, and share your talents as capably, constructively, and imaginatively as possible. That's a great life anthem!

If we are to help our clients achieve their outcomes, let's build that ability by ensuring we also achieve *ours*... in the largest sense possible.

World tour

- Decide on the mix you want your life to have between its various facets: work, family, leisure, experiences, all of it.

- Structure your time to maximize results and enjoyment; eliminate messes that distract from either.

- Create ways for your family to be a part of your global growth.

- Choose emotional attitudes that produce the results you want.

- Ask better questions; always find ways to create possibility.

- Manage your energy to deliver the most value to yourself and your clients.

- Make a life, and make it the one you want to lead.

Best Ways to Travel

By "best," we mean either most luxurious, most effective, or most fun and intriguing, each for the need or mood of the moment. We take it that which is which will be self-evident in what follows.

Planes

- Private jets are the most convenient way to travel. But a round-trip New York to Miami is about US$24,000. This becomes cost-effective if time is of the essence, and you are sharing this with, say, four colleagues.
- Businessjetseats.com is a new service purporting to sell "seats" on private-jet flights. This costs about double first class, the flights and times aren't always convenient, but it's worth checking out.

Best airlines (for first class and business class, not in order):

- Singapore Airlines: Offers the ability to order a meal before you fly on first class out of Singapore, the "Singapore Girl," a.k.a. the amazingly service-responsive air hostesses, exceptional on-time record, and if the A-380 stops having teething troubles their incomparable first class "suites"). The restrooms in first class are cleaned after each use.
- Virgin Atlantic: Pick-up and drop-off service at each end by limo, expedited check-in in London circumventing traditional

security and immigration, amazing lounges, standup bar on board, a seat that does a ballet into a full bed with a duvet, a blanket, and a thick pillow.

- British Airways: First-class seats that become flat beds, and if it works, Terminal 5 in Heathrow—at this moment decidedly *not* working.
- Lufthansa: Wonderful seats and the amazing private first-class terminal in Frankfurt with private car transfer to and from the plane.
- Cathay Pacific: Great pajamas and best flights from East Asia to the U.S.
- Qantas: Friendliness, good cuisine, even better first-class seats than BA.
- Emirates: Pick-up and drop-off service, private check-in in Dubai, mini-first-class suites with more to come on the A-380, best direct flight between New York and the Middle East.
- *Note: be careful about code sharing. You can find yourself on what was billed as an Air New Zealand flight run by Lufthansa and staffed by Alitalia. Never good.*

Trains

- The great train journeys of the world with plush private accommodation, extraordinary dining, in some cases wonderful entertainment, a chance to re-experience some of the splendor of the past traveling through some of the world's most stunning locations: The Venice-Simplon Orient Express (between London and Venice—the British Pullmans do the first portion of the trip), The Eastern and Oriental Express (between Singapore and Bangkok), The Royal Scotsman, The Palace on Wheels (through Rajasthan, India), The Canadian, and The Blue Train (in South Africa).
- The *Shinkansen* or "bullet train" through parts of Japan. Set your clock by it and enjoy smoked salmon and champagne as you travel. Or for that matter, opt for a Japanese *o-bento*.
- The TGV in France. When not on strike, timely, wonderful service.
- The Swiss train network. If you fly Swiss, it will even check your bags in at the train station! Elegant three-course meals with decent wine available.

- The Acela Express first-class car between Boston and Washington, DC, which is far more convenient than flights. Relax, get some work done, make calls, and leave and arrive from a city center.
- The Eurostar, under the Channel, London to Paris in a little more than two hours, from the center of both of these historic, yet also contemporary global cities.
- Wonderful subway systems, such as those found in Hong Kong, Tokyo, Singapore, and even London (in terms of making fast progress when the streets are congested or the weather makes taxis scarce).

Water travel

- Crossing the Atlantic on the *Queen Mary 2*, which has now supplanted the *Queen Elizabeth 2* on this route.
- Marvelous cruises, including the wonderfully intimate *Silversea*, on which caviar and champagne flow endlessly.
- The gondolas and water taxis of Venice.
- Dinner cruises down the Seine in Paris.
- The *abras* or water taxis in Dubai and elsewhere in the Middle East.
- An historic cruise down the Nile.
- Sailing on board a Chinese junk in Hong Kong.
- The Star Ferry in Hong Kong.
- For a bit of the bizarre, duck tours in amphibious landing vehicles in cities such as Boston, London, Singapore, and Dubai.
- A "bumboat" ride in Singapore.
- Sailing on a dhow in the Middle East.
- Kayaking through mangroves.
- Paddling through the floating markets in Bangkok.

Other noteworthy modes of travel

- Experiencing the expertise of the British cab drivers in their classic cabs.
- Carriage rides in places as far ranging as Central Park, Da Lat, Vietnam, Victoria, British Columbia, and Courcheval, France, during ski season.

- Cyclo tours in Hanoi, or *tuk-tuks* (small motorized vehicles that bob and weave between traffic) in Bangkok and elsewhere in Southeast Asia.
- Elephant rides in Vietnam, India, Thailand, and elsewhere in the region.
- Camel rides in the Middle East and northern Africa.
- Taking an escalator in the middle of a crowded thoroughfare in Hong Kong.
- Taking a tram from central Manhattan to Roosevelt Island. This quiet community overlooks the Manhattan skyline and makes for a good brief excursion.
- The Staten Island Ferry, the ultimate stunning "cheap date." It's free. On the return from Staten Island to Manhattan, you see the famous glittering skyline.
- The historic Peak Tram in Hong Kong.
- Being taken by carriage and buggy in Zermatt, Switzerland, where no cars are allowed.
- Helicopter rides to see famous skylines and landmarks over cities such as New York and Hong Kong, and over the various Hawaiian Islands, including dips into the volcano craters.

Our Favorite Hotels and Restaurants in Some of Our Favorite Cities

New York hotels

- The Carlyle: Art deco classic, stylish suites, fine dining, the historic. Bemelman's Bar and the Café Carlyle, where Bobby Short held sway and you can still hear the best café performers.
- The Four Seasons: Architectural paean to Gotham, stunning views, sixty-second-filling bathtubs, superb breakfasts.
- The Palace: Grand elegance, wonderfully intimate Concierge tower, huge suites overlooking St. Patrick's or the East River.
- The Mandarin Oriental: Large and lavish part of the Time Warner Center complex, with some of the country's best restaurants as its neighbors.
- The Peninsula: Part of the great chain, serves high tea, very European in the heart of Manhattan.
- The Michelangelo: In the heart of the theater district, a very European place within walking distance of every Broadway play and a hundred outstanding restaurants.

New York restaurants

- Per Se: Thomas Keller's showpiece, arguably the best wining and dining in the country.
- Daniel: The very best of classic French fine dining in a grand and elegant dining room.

- Le Bernardin: Sublime seafood converted into a fine dining extravaganza, but beware the occasional failed meal.
- Jean Georges: The flagship of one of the few masters of fine dining fusion.
- Del Posto: Babbo meets Felidia (two fine restaurants in their own right) and produces this Italian showpiece with grand staircase, grand people watching, and an astonishing Italian wine list.
- Nobu: The other fusion master, blending Japanese and South American flavors (equally good at Nobu 57, uptown).
- Spice Market: Another Jean Georges restaurant with whimsical esthetics showcasing the myriad flavors of the street food of Asia.
- Beijing Duck House: Either of two locations, some of the best crackling skin and here also the moist flesh (in east Asia, it's all about the skin) that you'll find on these shores.
- Peter Lugar's: Cross the Williamsburg Bridge to this nineteenth-century temple to the Porterhouse, amid beer-hall surroundings and meticulously brusque (with a twinkle in their eyes) waiters, best steak in New York, but beware, no credit cards accepted.
- The River Café: Also in Brooklyn, on the water, great for lunch and dinner, with an outstanding brunch on Sunday, elegant yet informal.
- Gramercy Tavern: Timeless, never anything but a great meal, wonderful to take a client to or for an intimate meal.
- Bouley: Intimate and lovely, superb service, one of the great chefs operating in a city full of great chiefs.
- La Grenouille: Remains one of the finest French restaurants anywhere, graced by huge flower displays, graceful and attentive service, and amazing food. Great for pre-theater.

London hotels

- The Dorchester: Wonderfully restored classic, sweeping Hyde Park views.
- The Four Seasons Park Lane: The hardy perennial, with some of the best staff anywhere, soon embarking on a major restoration.

- The Ritz: The standard setter for "ritzy" elegance and sophisticated grandeur, dining room from a great liner, unsurpassed service.
- The Baglioni: Quiet, intimate, all-suite gem near Kensington Gardens, with a Maserati as the house car.
- 51 Buckingham Gate: Overseen by the Taj group, sophisticated and spacious serviced apartments with a very good spa.

London restaurants

- Le Gavroche: The Roux brothers preside at this exemplary classical French dining room.
- Gordon Ramsay: Here in his home turf, the volatile chef and his disciples produce remarkably imaginative French fare.
- Zuma: The aspirant to the Nobu throne, innovative takes on sushi, Kobe beef and more; have the tasting menu to get a sense of its range.
- Hunan: Despite the unassuming room, tops the lists each year for best Chinese in London; if you like spicy food, sit back, let the owners order, and stop them when you're full.
- Cinnamon Club: The converted Westminster Library, with exquisitely authentic modern Indian cuisine.
- Zafferano: The reigning champ for Italian fine dining in London.
- J.Sheekey: Arguably the best Dover sole in London, wonderful seafood as well as intriguing game dishes. In the heart of the Strand, perfect for pre-theater.
- Mosimann's: Top hotels can get you membership for the night at this superbly elegant, refined, and illustrious dining club.
- Les Trois Garcons: Perhaps the most eccentric and visually stimulating of all, with great food and drink: try the wine cellar if you have a group.
- La Caprice: Down the street from The Ritz, a perennial classic, all clean lines and great service.
- The Ivy: A bit long in the tooth but still great for pre-theater and people watching.
- Sketch: An hysterical and noisy place on several levels with fine food and unbelievable rest rooms: egg pods.
- The Guinea Grill: In Mayfair, a quick walk from The Ritz, you'll need reservations for the crowded dining rooms, but

outstanding for lunch. An informal pub in the front in case you can't get in.

Note: you can easily join a London gambling club without any annual dues or even appearance, but with good food and fun games of Las Vegas chance.

Paris hotels

- The Four Seasons George V: The legendary hotel lovingly restored and uplifted with Four Seasons flourish.
- Hotel de Crillon: Heads of state, ambassadors, the cognoscenti, the literati, the glitterati all flock here.
- The Ritz: Like its London compatriot, a heady presence on the Place de Vendome.
- Plaza Athene: Quiet, dignified, exquisite in fine details, with legendary chef Alain Ducasse's flagship restaurant.
- The Lancaster: For years, the preferred quiet hideaway and getaway of those who want luxurious appointments and intimate attention.

Paris restaurants

- Le Grand Vefour: Napoleon took Josephine there, the atmosphere is redolent of another era, and Guy Martin produces extraordinary classics.
- Alain Ducasse: Natural ingredients sumptuously married to produce both classic and provencal tastes at this justly feted headliner.
- Le Cinq: Perhaps the best pairing of stunning cuisine with remarkable wine from the global "world champion" sommelier who is in residence.
- Le Pre Catalan: Another sommelier world champion presides here as French cooking is redefined.
- La Tour D'Argent: Step into culinary history, be surrounded by indulgent aesthetics, and go for those famous ducks (each with their own identification number).
- Chez L'Ami Louis: The classic ever so slightly snooty French bistro, where fur coats are tossed in overhead bins, and the roast chicken with frites is a revelation.

- Jules Verne: At the Eiffel Tower, now run by Ducasse, watch as the stunning cuisine complements the eye-popping views.
- Le Cascade: In the Bois de Boulogne, it features a nine-course (or more) dinner that requires about three hours of your time and astounding stamina. The staff are offended if you don't finish everything in every course. Lovely waterfalls outside.

Istanbul hotels

- The Ciragan Palace Kempinski: On the shores of the Bosporus, wonderful Turkish *hammam*, classic restaurants, you are actually living in a palace!
- The Four Seasons: The original one in the old town converted from an old jail, quiet, elegant, with beautiful terrace meals and views.
- The Ritz-Carlton: Classic Ritz-Carlton finesse, sweeping views, lovely lounge, top-notch Turkish cuisine.

For the restaurants, we recommend you dine at any of the restaurants in these fine hotels. Go for Arabic *mezze*, the aromatic grills, and the syrupy sweets matched with fresh mint tea.

Dubai hotels

- Burj Al Arab: Over-the-top opulence at this iconic sail-shaped hotel, voluptuousness bordering on the excessive.
- Madinat Jumeirah: Collection of Arabian-style houses, so you live in a "hotel villa," linked by waterways navigated by water taxis, with many fine restaurants and bars throughout the complex.
- The One and Only Royal Mirage and Palace: Stylish splendor, excellent beach access, some of Dubai's best restaurants.
- Raffles Dubai: A promising and enchanting newcomer with its "basic" rooms being on the caliber of suites in most hotels.

Again, all the hotels named have memorable dining venues. However, we recommend you go to Al Qasr for one of the best Lebanese meals in your life when not enjoying specialties at them.

Bangkok hotels

- The Oriental: At 130 years of age, arguably the most awarded and recognized "grande dame" of them all, with a spa that set the standard worldwide, superb restaurants, and a prescient staff.
- The Banyan Tree: An all-suite hotel with stunning views and fine Thai cuisine, an offshoot of the world-renowned Phuket Banyan Tree.
- The Regent: You'll walk outside between rooms but inside are magnificent accommodations, including large suites with six rooms and grand pianos.

Other than the Thai food at the Banyan Tree, and the restaurants at The Four Seasons (formerly the Regent), you would be well advised to dine extensively at the Oriental. Namely:

- Lord Jim's: For breathtaking views and a breathtaking lunch-time buffet and elegant seafood dinners.
- Normandie: For some of the best French dining in Asia.
- China House: With master chefs from Hong Kong, excelling particularly in dim sum.
- Sala Rim Naam: For an experience of how the medley of flavors that make up Thai cuisine are meant to be blended.

Singapore hotels

- The Raffles: At 125-plus years of age, this national landmark is both a larger than life spectacle and for those who reside here for a time, an urbane, classic, and sophisticated residence.
- The Ritz-Carlton Millenia Singapore: Stunning rooms, an exceptional Club Level, gorgeous pool, some of the best sushi in the region, and bathtub rituals to soothe colds or stimulate libidos.
- The Four Seasons: Clubby, sumptuous, with attentive service, a lovely spa, and one of the best Chinese restaurants in town.
- The Fullerton: The other historical property, restored to a brilliant hospitality luster, close to the Singapore River, exquisitely charming.

Singapore restaurants

- The Raffles Grill: A remarkable fine dining venue on a par with some of the best in Paris.
- Au Jardin: Superb French cuisine while looking out on the Botanic Gardens, wonderfully romantic.
- Brazil Steakhouse: Go to the original one here, which is a great example of *churascaria*-style presentations.
- The Four Seasons Hotel Chinese restaurant: Cantonese fine dining near its zenith.
- Mezza-Nine: Food from nine food traditions, from Chinese to Japanese, to Indian, to Italian, to roasts and more. Choose your seat based on the cuisine you want, and dine around the world.
- The hawker stands, food courts, and ethnic restaurants in Little India, Chinatown, and more.

Hong Kong hotels

- The Peninsula: Approaching 90 years of age, quintessentially sophisticated, with landmark restaurants, top-notch spa, and exquisite suites with private butler service.
- The Four Seasons: A relative newcomer to the scene, open, airy and striking, with the best concierge team in town, private spa suites for sybarites, excellent dining.
- The Island Shangri La: Giant multistory mural you can enjoy from a glass elevator, large rooms, perfectly placed near Hong Kong Park and Pacific Place, some of Hong Kong's best restaurants.
- Mandarin Oriental: The original, oozing sophistication and finesse from every pore, bar, restaurant and outlet.
- The Intercontinental: A view of Hong Kong Harbor that is unsurpassed, and an unforgettable adventure during Christmas.

Hong Kong restaurants

- Gaddi's at the Peninsula: Grand, elegant, classical French dining at its best, with people you are sure are spies eating across the room.

- Chesa at the Peninsula: Best fondues in Asia.
- Imasa at the Peninsula: Tokyo-quality sashimi and sushi, beautiful red bean ice-cream.
- The Lobster Bar: Wonderful food, with wonderful cabaret performances at the Island Shang.
- Petrus: Extraordinary French cuisine atop the Island Shangri La, with extraordinary sweeping views.
- Summer Palace: At the Island Shang, unbeatable Peking duck and shark's fin with crab roe.
- Nicholini's: Some of the finest Italian food in Asia at the Conrad in a sumptuously appointed setting.
- M's at the Fringe: Go to this avant-garde favorite in particular for its suckling pig and passionfruit pavlova.

Shanghai hotels

- The Portman Ritz-Carlton: A genteel address reflecting the best of Western elegance amid Eastern grace, wonderful Club Floor and expansive suites.
- The Four Seasons: A downtown hotel with both classic and contemporary touches, with staff that help you navigate this city like a pro while cosseted in luxurious rooms.
- The St. Regis: Cosmopolitan, in the heart of Pudong, with private butlers, luxurious fabrics and excellent dining.

We recommend you dine at the historic Bund. Ask your hotel for recommendations. Equally tap the excellent restaurants at each of the hotels named.

Tokyo hotels

- The Four Seasons Marunouchi: Like your own private club in Tokyo, seamless, amazing views of the bullet train from your bathtub, exquisite suites.
- The Mandarin Oriental: Like its New York twin, large, splashy, yet with intimate spaces and great dining venues.
- The Park Hyatt: Made famous by the movie *Lost in Translation*, with a famous bar, and hi-tech yet highly comfortable rooms and suites.

- The Okura: The classic old-timer, luxuriant, subtle, a bastion of refined good taste from the suites to the dining outlets.

Tokyo restaurants

- Joel Robuchon: The legendary chef in a transplanted European-style manor house with multi-Michelin-starred cuisine.
- L'Atelier by Robuchon: It started in Tokyo, fine dining meets tapas and it works!
- Enoteca Pinchiorri: The offshoot of the Florentine Michelin-starred establishment that offers different levels of wine degustation to accompany your cuisine.
- Ukai-tei: *Teppanyaki* converted into over-the-top fine dining, with abalone, Kobe beef, truffled *risottos* as side dishes and more.
- Sushiko: One of the finest landmark *sushi* establishments (a 200-year-plus tradition here!), where everything is converted by the master chef from that morning's catch at the fish market to delight the palate.
- Kitcho: The landmark *kaiseki* (Imperial eats) restaurant; if you can't get in, ask your hotel for their recommended *kaiseki* restaurants—you'll have a private room, chefs cooking just for you, and private hostesses in attendance serving *sake* and choreographing your meal!
- Tip: If you want *tempura*, go to a *tempura* restaurant; ditto with *shabu shabu*, *yakitori*, or whatever your Japanese cuisine passion is. Only those not in the know go for restaurants in Japan that serve a bit of everything.

Australian hotels

- The Four Seasons in Sydney: Spectacular views of the harbor and opera house, typical attentive service and elegant surroundings.
- The Intercontinental in Sydney: Located in a former treasury building, it features a completely open air interior and a sense of being outside while you're inside, with a major park across the way.

- The Park Hyatt in Melbourne: An incredibly understated but elegant facility with superb service, a block from the amazing St. Joseph's Cathedral, which rivals Notre Dame.

Australian restaurants

These are hit or miss, and your best bets are informal seafood places recommended by locals. However, in Sydney, do try Mirror, located right on the harbor near the ferry docks, a modern, continental bastion.

Other great hotels in the world

- Chateau Frontenac, Quebec City, Canada: Stay in one of the turret rooms, and try to be in Quebec during winter carnival to watch the races across the St. Lawrence.
- Hotel Utah, Salt Lake City: Overlooks the Mormon Church headquarters, wondrous views, beautiful in the winter.
- Fujiya, Hakone, Japan: You can watch Mt. Fuji in the distance amidst traditional Japanese care, wonderful food, and an international clientele.
- The Lodge, Pebble Beach: Outstanding rooms with fireplaces beside one of the finest golf courses ever built, flirting dangerously with the Pacific Ocean.
- Four Seasons, Georgetown: They will remember your favorite wines and flowers whenever you return; you can walk through Georgetown, and are readily available for business or fun in Washington, D.C.
- Hotel Arts, Barcelona, Spain: An elegant, small hotel surrounded by the exquisite work of Gaudi and filled with very important people. (Alan was crushed against Princess Caroline of Monaco in the miniscule elevator.)
- Royal, Luxemburg: *The* hotel in this small country, great service, wonderful accommodations, in the midst of everything that matters.

- The Breakers, Palm Beach: One of the great vacation destinations in the world, with three pools, beachfront, elegance from another age, and a staff that will wet the hot sand with a hose when you need to walk on it.
- Guanahani, St. Barts: Private villas with pools, walk down the hill to the great beach, breakfast on the ocean, subtle and perfect service.
- Castle Hill Inn, Newport: The turret suite overlooks, with 270° splendor, the former site of the America's Cup races, with historic Newport and the marinas and mansions just ten minutes away.
- The Metropole, Hanoi: One of the great "grandes dames" of the past. Superb French fare and exquisite Vietnamese cuisine. The Bamboo Bar overlooking the pool is exquisite for a cigar, port, and a foot massage at the same time!
- The Four Seasons Langkawi: Pure unadulterated sybaritic bliss in private villas with pools, massages in the midst of the rainforest, stylish bars and top-notch cuisine, wonderful cruises—a real contender to the throne of the other superb resort here, the Datai. Why choose? Try both!

Vacation Glory

Omar's vacation spots

- Spend a week between Venice and Florence. Four days at the Cipriani, on its own island next to Venice proper or the Danieli, a Venetian palace in the midst of it all, enjoying the stunning beauty of the architecture, the art, the concerts, and the cuisine, is ambrosial. Absolutely spend an evening at the legendary Harry's Bar. Then head over to Florence for two days of immersion in the beginnings of the Renaissance (literally!), and wallowing in the Uffizi and dining at the remarkable Enoteca Pinchiorri. Finally, spend a couple of days at Villa San Michele (which Michelangelo helped design), now a glorious hotel in Fiesole, on a hill overlooking Florence.
- Walk through Provence. The U.K. tour operator Inn Travel will transport your bags while you walk (the walk is called "To the Pont du Gard"). You start in Uzes, which was the first duchy of France. After a day of rambles here and experiencing local artisans, you walk to Collias (about 10 miles) through stunning landscape that the Romans fell in love with. Two nights at a lovely small hotel with Michelin-starred cuisine, having rambles along the river Gordes, and you then walk (about ten miles) via the world's greatest surviving aqueduct, the Pont du Gard, to le Vieux Castillon, a Relais & Chateaux property on a hill. Finally, "recuperate" at the charming town of Cezanne and Emile Zola, Aix-en-Provence, at the legendary Villa Gallici.

- Take time in the rainforests of Langkawi, Malaysia. One of the world's finest resorts, the Datai, built among the rainforests, is found here. Resident naturalist Irshad, the poet laureate of the rainforest and mangrove swamps, leads entertaining tours that make this extraordinary ecosystem come to vivid life. You have the spa treatments at the Datai (you are in the middle of the rainforest as they pummel you to health), the views of forest, water, and mountains from the pool, one of the best wine lists in Asia, and superb Thai, Malay, and French cuisine to savor.

- Stay at the Ciragan Palace Kempinski in Istanbul, reveling in a city that is both Asia and Europe. Enjoy its exquisite *hammam* treatments; dine on lavish Turkish cuisine as the sun slowly dips—a true slice of wonder. With Bosporus cruises, visiting the amazing Hagia Sophia and the Blue Mosque, taking in the sights, sounds, smell, bustle, and spirit of this modern Muslim nation and EU contender, you are at a true crossroads of early Byzantium, Orthodox Christianity, the Ottoman Empire, and more.

- Take a long weekend in Paris. Stay at the stunning George V. Have cocktails in its lounge amid fourteenth-century tapestries; stroll the Champs–Elysees, and veer off to visit Napoleon's tomb; have a drink at Hemingway's Bar at the Ritz; float down the Seine on a luxury barge; visit Notre Dame and the Ile de la Cite where Paris began; wander through the Orsay and the Louvre; eat warm baguettes in the morning from a local baker; dine at some of the world's finest and most sophisticated restaurants or exquisite bistros; gape at the world-famous opera house that was the inspiration for the *Phantom of the Opera*; watch the most beautiful city in Europe light up at night, and more. Samuel Johnson said "If you are tired of London, you're tired of life." I say, "If you can't enjoy Paris, you *have* no life."

- Two nights in Tokyo at the Four Seasons Marunouchi, enjoying the *onsen* (mineral bath), *shiatsu*, visiting the Temple of Mercy (the one temple that didn't burn during the fire bombing of Tokyo) and walking the adjacent *dori* (street) buying up artifacts, visiting the history museum, hanging out in bustling Shinjuku, taking early morning walks along the perimeter of the Imperial Palace, dining on the varieties of

Japanese cuisine. Then, move on to Hakone, staying at an historic *ryokan* (Japanese inn) and enjoying the proximity to Mt. Fuji, finally by bullet train to Kyoto for a few days of the finest "imperial cuisine" (*kaiseki*) and a chance to savor old Japan.

- Hole up at the Aman in Phuket. The Aman resorts are at the highest end of the luxury food chain. With usually no more than 40 rooms and suites, this is as exclusive as it gets. Aman was launched at this breathtaking Phuket property. Adrian Zecha finds locations and says, "There should be a hotel here." Now there is, on a stretch of private beach dotted by private villas, many with their own lap pools and jacuzzis. Personal housekeepers look after you, you can dine at the exceptional restaurant, or have virtually anything prepared for you at your villa, including wonderful barbecue on your terrace. Have massages under swaying palms and enjoy what is certainly nepenthe for battered nerves.

- Do Rome two ways, with a bit of Umbria in between. First stay at the Cavalieri Hilton. Hilton has its name on it, but it's still the historic Cavalieri. There is a three-star Michelin restaurant, La Pergola which is to live for. This is a great base for visiting the Vatican and St. Peter's. Then run away to Umbria, to the charming town of Torgiano. Stay at the elegant but unassuming Tre Vasale. The chefs are brilliant; the pool overlooking the Umbrian countryside is beguiling. Wonderful for day trips to Assisi and Perugia. Then head back to Rome, stay more centrally at the St. Regis Grand. Make it over to the Colosseum, the Spanish Steps, little *trattorias* where delights like *pasta carbonara* were invented and other delights like *pasta amatriciana* evolved into Roman delicacies, in search of perfect *gelatos* while watching lovers embrace *"la dolce vita"* (the good life) at the gardens of the Villa Borghese.

- Take in a weekend in Manhattan. Start at the River Café on a Friday night as the lights of Manhattan come on in front of you, then move to jazz at Dizzy's or a show at the Café Carlyle. Try the lemon *ricotta* hotcakes at the Four Seasons the next morning. Then take a walk or carriage ride through Central Park. Afterward, visit the amazing Cloisters. Have lunch possibly at the Oyster Bar at Grand Central or at Sant Ambroeus uptown if you're running late. Then book an hour or so with the best tour guide in Manhattan, art historian and enthusiast Justin Ferate, for a patented introduction to the architecture of Grand Central. Shop in Soho or museum hop up Fifth Avenue. Try dinner at Picholine (arguably the best cheese tray in North America) overlooking Lincoln Center, and then head out for a performance. Sunday morning, enjoy a leisurely wander through Greenwich Village and brunch. That afternoon, a Broadway matinee, followed by farewell drinks at Del Frisco's—a great way to cap an unforgettable weekend.

- Head to the charming historic town of Niagara-on-the-Lake for the annual Shaw Festival. This is perfect for ardent theater buffs, because this is the only theater festival dedicated to the works of George Bernard Shaw and his contemporaries. Rent a charming house for a week, or stay at the lovely Queen's Inn; take over a suite and have a week of dining at surprisingly good winery restaurants, long walks along the escarpment, top-notch theater productions from one of the finest repertory companies in North America, wonderful mud baths at the spas, touring in vintage Bentleys and more, and then move on to the town of Stratford, Canada, for the excellent Shakespeare festival there and the charming restaurants and paddleboats down the river.

Alan's vacation spots

- Everyone falls in love in Venice, so be sure you go with someone acceptable in that category. It's impossible to get a bad meal, the gondoliers are from central casting, and you'll get a great dose of history, from Marco Polo's home to the Doge's Palace and Bridge of Sighs. The square floods and you walk on planks, but you can have lunch as the water washes up to the lowest tables, and there are few foods so grand as pasta in black squid ink.

- Rome is the eternal city, and you'll never forget it. Try the Excelsior on the Via Veneto. St. Peter's is rich in history and magnificent art, no matter what your beliefs or lack of them. You'll find churches that are built on ancient religious sites, so that by the time you're in the lowest excavation you're looking at icons of pagan gods thirty feet below a functioning Catholic

Church. Hadrian's Villa took 400 years to complete, which means he was using the same general contractor that I do.

- The Caribbean is a vacation area I have to include as one entry. Some of the best water recreation in the world is in the Caymans. St. Maarten has a dichotomous French/Dutch existence, making the whole better than the sum of the parts. St. Bart's has several ultra-luxury resorts, with private pools for each villa and US$25 million-dollar yachts anchored bumper to bumper in the harbor like a crowded movie parking lot. Tiny islands such as Nevis and Antigua provide solitude and beauty.
- Hong Kong is a great synthesis of Asian mysticism and Western capitalism. I've found very little difference in it since the British returned it to China. It is crowded and busy, but fascinating and insanely cosmopolitan. The InterContinental has a view of one of the four great bays in the world, where hundreds of ships avoid collision in a 24-hour version of demolition derby on the water. The Star Ferry is a great ride between Kowloon and Hong Kong. Sitting atop Repulse Bay gives you an ideal view of just what the British first saw hundreds of years ago when they arrived.
- Costa Rica is an increasingly popular clime. Tourists (and particularly Americans) are wonderfully received, the food is terrific, and the visitor has the choice of two great coasts (and oceans) and a rainforest in between. I know many people who have bought property there so that they can make regular returns.
- The south of Spain, particularly Marbella and Torremolinos. The latter provides wonderful access to the Moorish influence in Spain, the Alcazar in Seville and Alhambra in Granada, and great architecture. You are on the Mediterranean, and can quickly take a ferry to Tangiers in Morocco for a day trip. Marbella affords water, great food, and easy trips into the Andalusian mountains, where you can shoot skeet, try tiny, wonderful eateries, and arrive at lofty towns, bisected by hundred-foot chasms, with ceremonial and working bull rings. (Advisory: learn the history of bullfighting and why it is a cultural phenomenon, whether or not you approve of the practice.)
- The French countryside. Paris is a "must see," I admit, but not a "repeat see" in my countercultural opinion. The countryside, however, with a highway system that merely

connects villages (no interstate autobahns here) allows you to see a great deal in normal travel. Mt. St. Michel, in the west, having served as a jail and a great cathedral hewn out of impossible rock amid the greatest tidal changes in the world, is one of my modern wonders. Toward the north is Normandy and the famous invasion beach. In the south is Cannes, Nice, and Monaco. (Great trip: fly to Rome, then drive north on the west coast of Italy, through Ventimiglia, into Monaco and, thence, the French coast.)

- London. I've been there two dozen times, and never tire of this legendary center of Empire and current urbane hub. You can easily join a local gambling club. But do stay at The Ritz and have high tea. The Tower of London, Buckingham Palace, Windsor, and other trappings of royalty are more than tourist attractions. They are trips into history, rich in learning and enjoyment. Unlike years ago, good food abounds. (Great trip: take the Eurostar, premium first class, from London to Paris.)
- Australia. As I write this, I'm preparing for my eleventh trip. The Great Barrier Reef lives up to its billing, especially at a place like The Grand Hayman Resort. The outback is fascinating, but be aware that you can see a stupefying variety of exotic wildlife in many preserves not far from Melbourne, including platypuses, dingos, koalas, and others. I had to referee a fight between a wallaby and a child over a bag of chips. Sydney has wonderful cultural opportunities, fine food, and another of the four great harbors of the world.
- I'll include one in the U.S., and that is God's country: Nantucket. It's expensive and busy, but there are beaches that are largely empty, the opportunity to drive off-road nearly into the Atlantic, superb food, and wonderful atmosphere. If you can, take the ferry from Hyannis. The best spot: the Wauwinet inn, with the bay on one side and the ocean on the other. You feel like you're a character in *The Great Gatsby*.

Index

Acclimatization day, need for, 54, 58, 63, 129
Airlines, *See* Planes
Alliance, *See also* Local alliance
  alliance partners, 17–18, 38
  subcontractor versus, 37–38
Aman in Phuket, vacation spots, 215
American-influenced business world, 12–15
  American clothing, 14
  American dollar, as the currency standard, 12–13
  American English, dominance, 12–15
  American-style democracy, 13–14
  cross-border consultancy, 14
Anti-jetlag preventives, 63
Arrogance, 166–169
Australia, 218
  hotels, 209–210
  vacation spots, 218

Baggage, light baggages, advantages, 55
Bangkok hotels, 206
  The Banyan Tree, 206
  The Oriental, 206
  The Regent, 206
British Airways, 198

Cabs, 199
Camel rides, 200
Capitalism, 10–11
  alliance partners, 17–18
  basis, 16
  collaboration compelled by, 15–18
  as the Esperanto of economics, 15
  in maintaining relationships, 16–17
  subcontractor, 17
Carriage rides, 199
Cathay Pacific, 198
Celebrations, participation in, importance, 138–140
Ciragan Palace Kempinski in Istanbul, vacation spots, 214
Clients, choice, 174–175
Clothing, importance, 63–65
  women, 64
Coaching approach, creating value space, 89–90
Collaboration
  capitalism compelling, 15–18
  conceptual collaborations, 17
Collins, Jim, 95
Commonalities
  negative, 10–11
  positive, 9–10
Connectivity
  maintaining, 24–27
  shared executive offices, 26
  through associates, 25–26
  through dialogues, 24–25
  ways to, 24–27
Contacts
  building, 16–27
  maintaining, 24–27

Contingency plans, preparing, 58–59
Continuing sale of oneself, 165–178
  clients, choice, 174–175
  feedback, 175–177
  global friendships, 170–173
  progress, importance, 177–178
  self-esteem, 166–170
Costa Rica, vacation spots, 217
Creative contention importance, 136
Cross-border consultancy, 7–12,
  14–15
Cultural adaptation, 135
Cultural distinctions
  adding value across, 133–145
  celebrating together, 138–140
  getting tuned to interactive
    atmosphere, 135–138
  reasons to ignore, 140–145
Customer business
  acquisition, 39
  delivery, 39
  methodology, 39
Cyclo tours, 200

Delivery people, 16
Disparity belief in global market,
  failures, 8–11
Drucker, Peter, 8, 14, 33–35, 81, 91
Dubai hotels, 205
  Burj Al Arab, 205
  Madinat Jumeirah, 205
  The One and Only Royal Mirage
    and Palace, 205
  Raffles Dubai, 205

Easy mode of business, for success,
  97–98
Economies change and payments,
  151
Educating yourself for
  success, 69–84
  basics, 70–74
  continual education, need
    for, 69–70
  educating habits, global credibility,
    83–84

  lifelong learning, 79–83
  understanding countries and
    people, 74–79
Ego, 168–169
Elephant rides, 200
Emerson, Ralph Waldo, 165
Emirates, 42, 52, 63, 198
Emotional balance, 184–188
Emotional well-being,
  importance, 64
Energy balance, 191–194
Escalator, 200
Expenses, payments for
  reasonable expenses, 155–156
Expertise, projecting,
  See Projecting expertise

Family balance, 184–188
Feedback, 175–177
Flights, choice of, 52–53
Florence, vacation spots, 213
Foreign exchange fluctuations, 151
Fresh view, need for, 10–11
Friendships, global, advantages,
  171–173

Getting paid, *See* Payments
Global market
  disparity belief, failures, 8–11
  influencing behavior, 7
Global routes, advantages, 5–18
Grooming, importance, 64–65

Helicopter rides, 200
Hill, Napoleon, 34
Hong Kong
  hotels, 207
    The Four Seasons, 207
    The Intercontinental, 207
    The Island Shangri La, 207
    Mandarin Oriental, 207
    The Peninsula, 207
  restaurants, 207–208
    Chesa at the Peninsula, 208
    Gaddi's at the Peninsula, 207
    Imasa at the Peninsula, 208

The Lobster Bar, 208
M's at the Fringe, 208
Nicholini's, 208
Petrus, 208
Summer Palace, 208
vacation spots, 217
Hotels, favorite hotels, *See also*
     Australia: hotels; Bangkok
     hotels; Dubai hotels; Hong
     Kong: hotels; Istanbul hotels;
     London: hotels; New York
     hotels; Paris: hotels; Shanghai
     hotels; Singapore: hotels; Tokyo:
     hotels
The Breakers, Palm Beach, 211
Castle Hill Inn, Newport, 211
Chateau Frontenac, Quebec City,
     Canada, 210
choices for smoother businessm,
     53–54
The Four Seasons Langkawi, 211
Four Seasons, Georgetown, 210
Fujiya, Hakone, Japan, 210
Guanahani, St. Barts, 211
Hotel Arts, Barcelona, Spain, 210
Hotel Utah, Salt Lake City, 210
The Lodge, Pebble Beach, 210
The Metropole, Hanoi, 211
required features, 53–54
Royal, Luxemburg, 210
Human software for global
     consulting, 165–178, *See also*
     Continuing sale of oneself

Impact
of brand and presence, amplifying,
     27–31
adapting to local needs, 27–31
maximizing, 19–31
Integrity, 169–170
International presence,
     creating, 33–47
local publishing, 35
local selling, 36–37
local, formal office, 44–47
physical presence, 40–44

products launching in print and
     audio, 36–37
speak locally, 35
teleconferences, 35
through local alliance, 37–40
video tapes, 36
Internet
advantages, 6
global interface creation by, 6
iPhone, usage tips, 67n3
Istanbul hotels, 205
The Ciragan Palace Kempinski,
     205
The Four Seasons, 205
The Ritz-Carlton, 205

Jetlag, managing, 62–63

Knowledge export,
     importance, 33–48

Langkawi, vacation spots,
     Malaysia, 214
Lee Kuan Yew, 29–30, 140
Life balance, 179–195
emotional balance, 184–188
energy balance, 191–194
family balance, 184–188
making a life, 194
mental balance, 188–191
time balance, 180–184
Lifelong personal education, 79–83
Local alliance, in creating
     international presence, 37–40
Local publishing, in creating
     international presence, 35
Local, formal office
in creating international
     presence, 44–47
physical office, drawbacks,
     44–46
London, 218
hotels, 202–203
     51 Buckingham Gate, 203
     The Baglioni, 203
     The Dorchester, 202

The Four Seasons Park Lane, 202
The Ritz, 203
restaurants, 203
   Cinnamon Club, 203
   Gordon Ramsay, 203
   Hunan, 203
   J.Sheekey, 203
   La Caprice, 203
   Le Gavroche, 203
   Les Trois Garcons, 203
   Mosimann's, 203
   Sketch, 203
   The Guinea Grill, 203
   The Ivy, 203
   Zafferano, 203
   Zuma, 203
vacation spots, 218
Lufthansa, 198

Mackay, Harvey, 27
Manhattan, vacation spots, 215
Markets, 22–24
   entering, 22
   expansion, 22
Material, requisite for success, 51–67
   contingency plans, preparing,
      58–59
   Jetlag managing, 62–63
   joining business clubs, 58
   light traveling, advantages, 55
   limo transportation, 53
   local materials, providing, 57–58
   local support and help, 65–66
   maintaining mental fitness, 52–65
   maintaining physical fitness, 52–65
   meeting times and dates,
      scheduling, 58
   personal belongings to carry,
      56–57
   personal image management,
      63–65
   scheduling acclimatization days, 54
   site selection for meetings, 58
   top-rated hotels, 53–54
   traveling ways, 52
   virtual assistants, 61–62
   virtual offices, 62

Mental balance, 188–191
Mental fitness, maintaining ways,
   52–65

Nabokov, Vladimir, 69
Need for global consulting, 5–18
Negative consulting commonalities,
   10–11
Networking, 24–27, *See also*
   Connectivity
New paradigms, prerequisite for
   success, 85–115
   building momentum, 91–94
   delivering value, 94–97
   easy mode of business, 97–98
New value creation, 86–89
New York hotels, 201
   The Carlyle, 201
   The Four Seasons, 201
   The Mandarin Oriental, 201
   The Michelangelo, 201
   The Peninsula, 201
   The Palace, 201
New York restaurants, 201–202
   Beijing Duck House, 202
   Bouley, 202
   Daniel, 201
   Del Posto, 202
   Gramercy Tavern, 202
   Jean Georges, 202
   La Grenouille, 202
   Le Bernardin, 202
   Nobu, 202
   Per Se, 201
   Peter Lugar's, 202
   The River Café, 202
   Spice Market, 202
Niagara, vacation spots, 216

Online traveling plans, drawbacks,
   59–61

Paris
   hotels, 204
      Hotel de Crillon, 204
      The Four Seasons
         George V, 204

The Lancaster, 204
Plaza Athene, 204
The Ritz, 204
restaurants, 204–205
Alain Ducasse, 204
Chez L'Ami Louis, 204
Jules Verne, 205
La Tour D'Argent, 204
Le Cascade, 205
Le Cinq, 204
Le Grand Vefour, 204
Le Pre Catalan, 204
vacation spots, 214, 217–218
Payments, 149–163
charging guidelines, 157–158
delays, 151–152
economies change, 151
express lane, 160–163
philosophical, 160–161
pragmatic, 162–163
process, 161–162
foreign exchange fluctuations, 151
reasonable expenses, 155–157
terms of endearment, 152–155
contingent actions, 155
preventive actions, 153–154
usual suspects, round up,
149–150
Personal, requisite for success,
69–84, See also Educating
yourself for success
image management, 63–65
personal belongings to
carry 56–57
cell phone, 56–57
laptop, 56
USB device, 57
Physical fitness, maintaining ways,
52–65
Physical presence, 40–44
Physical travel, importance, 8
Planes, traveling way, 197–200
British Airways, 198
Cathay Pacific, 198
Emirates, 198
Lufthansa, 198
private jets, 197

Qantas, 198
Singapore Airlines, 197
Virgin Atlantic, 197–198
Positive consulting commonalities,
9–10
Private jets, 197
Projecting expertise, 19–31,
See also International presence
ways to, 19–21
focussing, 20
getting the right type, 19–21
Provence, vacation spots, 213

Qantas, 198

Reasonable expenses, 155–157
Reframe technique, 136
Relationships, building, 16–17,
19–31, See also Impact
maintaining connections, 24–27,
See also Connectivity
Representation, in creating presence,
44–47
Restaurants, favorite restaurants,
201–211, See also Hong Kong:
restaurants; London: restaurants;
New York restaurants; Paris:
restaurants; Singapore:
restaurants; Tokyo: restaurants
Retainers fees, criteria for, 130–131
Rome, vacation spots, 215–216

Self-care, importance, 52–55
Self-esteem, 166–170
arrogance, 168–169
confidence, 168
ego, 168–169
ingredient of, 167
Shanghai hotels, 208
The Four Seasons, 208
The Portman Ritz-Carlton, 208
The St. Regis, 208
Singapore
hotels, 206
The Four Seasons, 206
The Fullerton, 206
The Raffles, 206

The Ritz-Carlton Millenia
Singapore, 206
restaurants, 207
Au Jardin, 207
Brazil Steakhouse, 207
Mezza-Nine, 207
The Four Seasons Hotel
Chinese restaurant, 207
The Raffles Grill, 207
Singapore Airlines, 92, 135–136,
197
Socialization, importance, 41
Society understanding of,
importance, 75
Spain, vacation spots, 217
Stress, 187
Subcontractors, 17
alliance versus, 37–38

Taylor, Dan, 95–96
'Divorce Mediation Solution', 96
'Parent Care Solution', 96
Technology
in maintaining connectivity, 24–27
Teleconferences, 35
Think and Grow Rich, 34
Time balance, 180–184
Tokyo
hotels, 208–209
The Four Seasons Marunouchi,
208
The Mandarin Oriental, 208
The Okura, 209
The Park Hyatt, 208
restaurants, 209
Enoteca Pinchiorri, 209
Joel Robuchon, 209
Kitcho, 209
L'Atelier by Robuchon, 209
Sushiko, 209
Tip, 209
Ukai-tei, 209
vacation spots, 214
Trains, 198–199
Trams, 200
Transportation
choices for smoother business, 53

Travel/Traveling, *See also* Physical
travel
choices for smoother
business, 52–53
importance, 40–44
modes of, 197–200, *See also*
Planes; Trains; Water travel
cabs, 199
Camel rides, 200
carriage rides, 199
cyclo tours, 200
elephant rides, 200
escalator, 200
Helicopter rides, 200
tram, 200
productive ways to, 41–43
combining visits, 41
light travel, 42
necessary products, 43
planning the stay, 42
travel agents, importance, 59–61
Vacation spots, 213–218
Aman in Phuket, 215
Australia, 218
Ciragan Palace Kempinski in
Istanbul, 214
Costa Rica, 217
Florence, 213
Hong Kong, 217
Langkawi, Malaysia, 214
London, 218
Manhattan, 215
Niagara, 216
Paris, 214, 218
Provence, 213
Rome, 215–216
Spain, 217
Tokyo, 214
Venice, 213, 216
Value, creation, 86–89
personal participation, 88
Value-based fees/pricing
advantages, 120–121, 126–127
applying, 119–132
converts, creating, 126–129
formula, 121
fundamentals of, 123–126

objectives, establishing, 123
project value, establishing,
    124–126
success metrics, establishing,
    123–124
internationally using, 129–131
  labor intensity, reducing,
    129–130
  retainers, using, 130–131
  RFPs, overcoming, 130–131
  rigid procurement policies,
    overcoming, 130–131
objections, overcoming, 126–129
philosophy of, 119–122
setting, basis, 123–126
Venice, vacation spots, 213, 216
Video tapes
  in creating international presence, 36

Virgin Airlines, 52, 143
Virgin Atlantic, 73, 197–198
Virtual assistants, 61–62
Virtual offices, 62
Virtual presence creation
  ways to, 24–27
    dialogues, 24–25

Water travel, 199
Websites
  citibanksucks.com, 6
  global interface creation by, 6
  My3Cents.com, 6
Weiss, Alan, 5, 15, 18n2, 119
Women business travelers, 64
Work/life balance, *See* Life balance
World market for consulting
  services, 5–8